THE Greatest Of All Time

CLEAN JOKES

for Kids

THE Greatest Of All Time
CLEAN JOKES
for Kids

Funny Stories,
Riddles,
Knock-Knocks,
and More!

BARBOUR
kidz

A Division of Barbour Publishing

Editorial assistance by Ruthanah Gaston

Print ISBN 978-1-64352-984-4

Published by Barbour Publishing, Inc., 1810 Barbour Drive, Uhrichsville, Ohio 44683, www.barbourbooks.com

Our mission is to inspire the world with the life-changing message of the Bible.

ecpa Member of the
Evangelical Christian
Publishers Association

Printed in the United States of America.
000896   0821   BP

INTRODUCTION

*A merry heart doeth
good like a medicine*
PROVERBS 17:22

Need a dose of that "merry heart medicine"? Well, here's a heapin' helpin' for kids ages 8 to 12!

Here are scores of funny stories, riddles, and knock-knocks covering nearly every aspect of life:

- church
- school
- sports
- parents and siblings
- Fido and Fluffy
- and much, much more

They're all good clean fun—the kind of stuff you could share with grandma. You'll even find space for capturing your own favorite jokes and stories.

It's the GOAT—the greatest of all time!

A helicopter pilot was running out of gas and hovered over a desert. He saw a group of hikers below and made a sign reading, WHERE AM I? He held the sign up to the window so the hikers could read it.

The hikers quickly made a sign of reply. They held it up for the pilot to read. It said, YOU'RE IN A HELICOPTER.

> **What's as big as an elephant but doesn't weigh an ounce?**
>
> *An elephant's shadow.*

JON: "My parents just got a new computer for my sister."

RON: "I wish my parents could make that kind of trade for my sister."

During a medical emergency, a young man brought his wife to a small-town doctor's office. The nurses escorted the woman to the examination area, and the husband anxiously took a seat in the lobby.

For the next few minutes, he could hear the doctor bark out an unsettling string of orders to the staff. First it was "Screwdriver!" Then, "Knife!" Then, "Pliers!" When he heard, "Sledgehammer!" the young man couldn't take any more. He burst into the examination room and shrieked, "Doctor, what's wrong with her?"

"We have no idea," the doctor said. "Right now, we're still trying to open the medicine cabinet."

Why did the man stare intently at the can of orange juice?

Because it said "concentrate."

"Mommy, Randall just broke the bedroom window!"

"Oh, no! How did that happen?"

"I threw a shoe at him, and he ducked."

What did Noah do for a living?

He was an ark-itect.

TEACHER: "If you had one dollar and you asked your father for another, how many dollars would you have?"

BOY: "One dollar."

TEACHER: "Sorry, you don't know your arithmetic."

BOY: "You don't know my father."

NEWS ANCHOR: "So what's the chance of rain today?"

METEOROLOGIST: "Oh, no worse than 50 percent."

ANCHOR: "And what's the chance you're wrong?"

METEOROLOGIST: "About the same."

What did the mother buffalo say to her boy as he was leaving?

"Bison."

A man made a call to his travel agent's office. "How long will it take to fly from here to Syracuse?" he asked.

"Um, just a minute," answered the agent.

"Wow! That isn't long at all! Thank you," he said, then hung up.

> **Why shouldn't you take your computer into rush-hour traffic?**
>
> *Because it might crash.*

Two truck drivers came to a low bridge. The clearance sign said 10 feet 8 inches. When they got out and measured their truck, they discovered their vehicle was eleven feet. The first man looked at the other and said, "I can't see any cops around. Let's go for it!"

> **What is the fastest way to annoy a doctor?**
>
> *Take away his patients.*

> **What is a bird's favorite food?**
>
> *Chocolate-chirp cookies.*

BOB: "You know what your main golf problem is?"

TED: "What?"

BOB: "You stand too close to the ball after you've hit it."

> **What can you always find to eat if you're shipwrecked on a desert island?**
>
> *Lots of* sand-*wiches.*

A man was seated on an airplane, preparing for his first flight. As he buckled his seat belt, he turned to the woman seated next to him and asked, "Would you happen to know about how often jetliners like this crash?"

After a brief pause, she answered, "Usually only once."

EMPLOYEE: I've worked here for over twenty years and have never asked for a raise.

EMPLOYER: That's why you've worked here for twenty years.

Why do porcupines never lose games?

Because they always have more points than any other animal.

TEACHER: "Where are the Great Plains?"
SAM: "At the great airports!"

Did you hear about the man who crashed the helicopter?

He was getting cold, so he turned off the fan.

Why did the college graduate
go to work at the bank?

He heard there was money in it.

Hickory dickory dock,
The mice ran up the clock,
The clock struck one,
And the others escaped with
minor injuries.

What is a woodpecker's
favorite kind of joke?

A knock-knock joke.

ROB: When you saw the guy driving
toward you, why didn't you give him half
the road?

BOB: I couldn't tell which half he
wanted!

HEARD ANOTHER GREAT JOKE? WRITE IT HERE!

HA HA HA

HA

....

....

....

....

....

....

....

....

ED: I have a job in a watch factory.

MIKE: Oh really? What do you do?

ED: I just stand around and make faces.

> **What would you call a snake
> that drinks too much coffee?**
>
> *A hyper viper.*

A famous doctor was being interviewed by the press. Looking to spice things up a little, one reporter asked if the doctor had ever made any serious mistakes.

"Well, yes," he sighed. "I once cured a billionaire."

"How was that a mistake?" the reporter asked.

The doctor shook his head wearily. "I did it in one visit!"

> **Why were the birds punished?**
>
> *For using fowl language.*

TIM: "I've heard bears won't chase you at night if you carry a flashlight."

KIM: "Depends on how fast you carry it."

Why did the m&m go to college?
It wanted to be a Smartie.

A frantic nurse ran into the doctor's office. "That man you just gave a clean bill of health to has dropped dead just outside the hospital door. What are we going to do?"

"Quick!" the doctor told the nurse. "Turn him around so it looks as if he was coming in and just didn't get here in time!"

NELL: "Is it true that ants are the hardest-working creatures?"

SCIENCE TEACHER: "That's what a lot of scientists believe."

NELL: "Then why are they always attending picnics?"

What kind of animal always is found at baseball games?

The bat.

How is business?

TAILOR: Oh, it's sew-sew.

ELECTRICIAN: It's fairly light.

AUTHOR: All write.

FARMER: It's growing.

ASTRONOMER: Looking up!

ELEVATOR OPERATOR: Well, it has its ups and downs.

TRASH COLLECTOR: It's picking up.

> ### Why can't car mufflers participate in marathon races?
>
> *They're too exhausted.*

A man seated on an airplane discovered two engines on one side were on fire. He began to holler, "Two engines on fire! Two engines on fire!"

The passengers began to panic.

Suddenly the pilot ran from the cockpit with a parachute on his back. "Don't worry!" he yelled. "I'm going for help!"

> ### Where do polar bears vote?
>
> *The North Poll.*

A doctor's receptionist answered the phone and was screamed at by an excited man at the other end of the line.

"My wife's in labor!" he yelled. "I think she's going to deliver any minute now."

"Please calm down," the receptionist said. "Try to relax and give me some basic information. Is this her first child?"

"No, no! I'm her husband!"

What should you wear to Thanksgiving dinner?

A har-vest.

"My feet are sore," one bear said to another. "I'm going to the mall to buy tennis shoes."

"What for?" asked his friend. "You're still going to have bear feet."

> ### What's an auto mechanic's favorite kind of candy?
>
> *Car-amels.*

A man in a swimming pool was on the very top diving board. He lifted his arms and bent his knees and was about to dive when an attendant came running up, shouting, "Don't dive! There's no water in that pool."

"That's all right," said the man. "I can't swim."

KENDALL: "Mommy, there's a woman at the door with a baby."

MOM: "Well, tell her we don't need any more."

> **What did the dentist of the year get at the awards ceremony?**
>
> *A plaque.*

When little Josie came home from her first day at school, her mother asked, "So how do you like school, Josie?"

"Closed," Josie said.

Who stole soap from the bathtub?

The robber ducky.

AL: I caught a twenty-pound salmon last week.

SAL: Were there any witnesses?

AL: There sure were. If there weren't, it would have been forty pounds.

Why did the tire get fired from its job?

It couldn't stand the pressure.

TEACHER: "How can one child make so many mistakes in one day?"

STUDENT: "By getting up early."

Why did the boy put
candy under his pillow?

To have sweet dreams.

BRAD: "Why do bears paint their faces yellow?"

LAD: "Don't know."

BRAD: "So they can hide in banana trees."

LAD: "Impossible. I've never seen a bear in a banana tree."

BRAD: "That's because they've painted their faces yellow."

Did you hear about the spider that
enrolled in computer courses?

It wanted to design web pages.

Sherlock Holmes and Dr. Watson were on a camping and hiking trip. The first night out they had gone to bed and were lying looking up at the sky. "Watson," Holmes said, "look up. What do you see?"

"Well, I see thousands of stars."

"And what does that mean to you?"

"Well, I guess it means we will have another nice day tomorrow. What does that mean to you, Holmes?"

"To me, it means someone has stolen our tent."

HEARD ANOTHER GREAT JOKE? WRITE IT HERE!

HA HA HA HA

....

....

....

....

....

....

....

....

....

MARIA: "My school class has adopted a talking bird!"

PATSY: "That's nothing. My class has a spelling bee."

Why did the computer go to the doctor?

It had a virus.

Knock-knock.
Who's there?
Kenya.
Kenya who?
Kenya gimme a dollar
to buy a pack of gum?

Did you hear the joke about the roof?

Never mind, it's over your head.

How do you tell a chili pepper from a bell pepper?

The chili pepper always wears a jacket.

An eighth grader was visibly frustrated as he struggled with his homework. Finally, he slammed the textbook shut, threw down his pencil, and announced to his parents, "I've decided I'm a conscientious objector."

"Why did you decide that?" his father asked.

"Because wars create too much history."

Heard about the guy who had to quit his job due to illness and fatigue?

His boss was sick and tired of him.

"But why can't I talk
inside the library?"
Mandy asked her
mother.

"Because you
have to be quiet.
Noise is a distraction.
The people around
you can't read."

"Can't read? Then why are they at the
library?"

> **What's black and white and red all over?**
> *A blushing zebra.*

A class of paratroopers was ready for its jump. After the troopers jumped from the plane, they opened their chutes. One late jumper streaked past them with the handle of the ripcord loose in his hand.

"Hey, are you okay?" yelled his buddy.

> **Why doesn't bread like warm weather?**
> *It gets too toasty.*

"So far!" he shouted. What kind of computers wear shades?

The ones that have Windows.

How did the bubble gum cross the road?
On the bottom of the chicken's foot!

What has a fork and a mouth but never eats food?

A river.

The flight attendant was pointing out to passengers that their seats could be removed and used as flotation devices. One woman, on her first flight, said, "I'd prefer to be sitting on a parachute!"

What can't you eat for breakfast?

Lunch and dinner.

CHUCK: Did you hear about the trapeze performer who fell to the ground?

BUCK: Did he hit a net first?

CHUCK: Yes, and Annette wasn't too happy about it.

What's the tiniest room you'll ever find?
A mushroom.

"Oooo! This wind is terrible," said Jodi. "It made a total mess of my hair."

"Yeah," agreed Lilly. "You look like you've been through a hairicane."

Why didn't Mom pay the telephone bill?
She believed in free speech.

Two fleas were walking out of a theater when they discovered it was raining hard. "Shall we walk?" said one flea.

"No," said the other. "Let's take a dog."

Why did the archaeologist go bankrupt?

Because his career was in ruins.

A husband raced into his house. "I've found a great job!" he exclaimed to his wife. "The pay is incredible, they offer free medical insurance, and give three weeks' vacation!"

"That does sound wonderful," said the wife.

"I'm glad you think so," replied her husband. "You start tomorrow."

Why are frogs so happy?

They eat whatever bugs them.

A young boy was watching the news with his mother. There was a report on an airline crash, and he asked her about the "black box" that was mentioned.

"It contains a record of the plane's information right up until the crash," she explained to him.

"Isn't it destroyed when the plane hits the ground?" asked the boy.

"No. It's made of a very strong metal that protects it."

Lowering his brow, the boy asked, "Why don't they make the airplane out of that?"

What do you get when you put a kitten in a scanner?

A copycat.

POLLY: "Why are you wearing all those clothes to go paint the fence?"

AGNES: "The can says you need two coats to do a good job."

HEARD ANOTHER GREAT JOKE? WRITE IT HERE!

HA HA HA HA

....
....
....
....
....
....
....
....

MISSY: "I just got a new pair of alligator shoes!"

SISSY: "I didn't know you had an alligator."

"What do you mean I'm not qualified?" demanded a job applicant. "I have an IQ of 150. I scored 1,480 on the SAT. I was magna cum laude in graduate school."

"Yes," replied the hiring supervisor, "but we don't really require intelligence around here."

Why did the farmer receive an award?

Because he was outstanding in his field.

"My Mom sure gets mean when she's in the kitchen," Scot said.

"What does she do?" asked Branden.

"She does things like beat the cake mix, mash the potatoes, whip the cream. . . ."

A doctor in a teaching hospital was discussing an X-ray with his students.

"This patient has been walking with a pronounced limp for some time," he said. "The X-ray shows us his fibula and tibia are radically arched."

He pointed to a student. "You—what would you do in this case?"

"Well, gee!" said the student. "I guess I'd limp too."

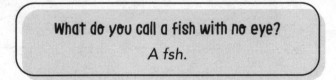

What do you call a fish with no eye?

A fsh.

DIRECTOR: Now, in this scene you jump off the cliff.

ACTOR: But suppose I get killed?

DIRECTOR: Don't worry—it's the last scene in the film.

What's the difference between a moldy vegetable and a depressing song?

One is a bad salad, and the other is a sad ballad.

Where do fish like to go on vacation?

Finland.

Why did the stork stand on one leg?

Because if he lifted the other leg, he'd fall.

Which month has 28 days?

All twelve of them, actually.

"When Abraham Lincoln was your age," a man said to his lazy teenage son, "he was chopping wood, plowing, and hunting for food."

"When he was your age," the boy responded, "he was president of the United States."

Before the discovery of Australia, what was the earth's largest island?

Australia.

What do you say when someone throws a goose at a duck?

"Duck, duck! Goose!"

What word contains three E's but only one letter?

Envelope.

How do you warm up a room after it's been painted?

Give it a second coat.

What has a head and a tail but no body?

A coin.

Knock-knock.
Who's there?
Stan.
Stan who?
Stan back.
I'm coming in.

Why did the photograph go to prison?

Because it was framed.

Two easterners were hunting in the Rocky Mountain wilderness when a huge grizzly bear sprang onto their path, reared up, and roared.

One hunter was terrified. The other kept his presence of mind and calmly instructed, "Don't move a muscle. Just stand like a statue, and the bear will get bored and go away."

"H–h–how do you know?"

"I read it in a book about the Lewis and Clark expedition."

They both stood motionless. The bear didn't go away but instead drew closer and roared more furiously.

The first hunter stammered, "I–I–I don't think the bear read that book!"

A man was purchasing a fancy pen and pencil set. "I suppose this is to be a surprise, sir?" asked the clerk.

"Oh, yes it is," replied the man. "It's my son's birthday, and he asked for a new car."

What do you call a bee that hums very quietly?

A mumblebee.

A man and his wife attended a dinner party at the home of their friends. Near the end of the meal, the wife reprimanded her husband. "That's the third time you've gone for dessert," she scolded. "The hostess must think you're an absolute pig."

"I don't think so," he said. "I've been telling her it's for you."

HEARD ANOTHER GREAT JOKE? WRITE IT HERE!

HA HA HA HA

....

....

....

....

....

....

....

....

....

DINER: Is there any stew on the menu?

WAITER: There was, but I wiped it off.

What kind of ears do you
find on a train locomotive?

Engineers.

A little boy showed his father a ten-dollar bill he had found in the street.

"Are you sure it was lost?" asked his father.

"Yes," answered the boy. "I saw the man looking for it."

What gives you the power
to walk through walls?

A door.

How many items can you put into an empty grocery bag?

One. After that, the bag isn't empty anymore.

A woman went to the pet shop to buy a parrot. When she picked out a rare breed, the owner congratulated her on her choice.

"If you'd like, I could send you the bill at the end of the month," said the pet shop owner.

"No, thanks," said the woman, "I'd like to take the whole bird today."

What has one head, one foot, and four legs?
A bed.

A woman who ran to the mall for a quick errand lost her purse, but an honest teenage boy returned it to her. The woman looked inside her purse and remarked, "That's really odd. Earlier I had a twenty-dollar bill inside, but now it's gone. Instead, I see four fives."

"Well," the boy explained, "the last time I found a lady's purse, she didn't have change for a reward."

CUSTOMER: When I bought this car, you guaranteed that you would fix anything that broke.

CAR DEALER: Yes, that's right.

CUSTOMER: Well, I need a new garage.

What has no mouth or teeth, but does have eyes?

A potato.

A man at the airline counter tells the woman behind the desk, "I'd like this bag to go to London, this one to Seattle, and this one to Quebec."

"I'm sorry, sir. We can't do that," she replied.

"I'm sure you can," he answered. "That's what you did the last time I flew with your airline."

Why do lobsters have a hard time sharing?
    Because they're shellfish.

What travels faster, heat or cold?

*Heat, because you
can easily catch cold.*

A tourist was driving down a desert road and came upon a sign that said, ROAD CLOSED. DO NOT ENTER. The man thought the road looked passable, so he ignored the sign and continued driving down the road. A mile later, he came to a bridge that was out. He turned around and drove back in the direction he came from. As he approached the warning sign, he read on the other side: WELCOME BACK. TOLD YOU SO!

What's the difference between a cat and a comma?

A cat has its claws at the end of its paws; a comma is a pause at the end of a clause.

Hew de baby birds learn te fly?

They wing it.

What did the driver say when she came to a fork in the road?

"This must be the place to eat."

Why de dragens sleep during the day?

So they can hunt knights.

"Look at that speed!" said one hawk to another as a jet-fighter plane zoomed over their heads.

"Hmph!" snorted the other. "You would fly fast too, if your tail was on fire!"

What's the difference between a tiger and a lion?

The tiger has the mane part missing.

What happens when a frog's car breaks down?

He gets toad away.

SWIMMER: Are you sure there aren't any sharks along this beach?

LIFEGUARD: Oh, yes, I'm sure. They don't get along well with the alligators.

Why did the doughnut maker retire?

He was fed up with the hole business.

What did the astronaut think of the takeoff?

She thought it was a blast.

HEARD ANOTHER GREAT JOKE? WRITE IT HERE!

HA HA HA

HA

Two barbershops were in red-hot competition. One put up a sign advertising haircuts for seven dollars. His competitor put up one that read, WE REPAIR SEVEN-DOLLAR HAIRCUTS.

The factory foreman inspected the shipment of crystal vases ready to leave the plant and approached his new packer. "I see you did what I asked: stamped the top of each box, THIS SIDE UP, HANDLE WITH CARE."

"Yes, sir," the worker replied. "And just to make sure it arrives safely, I stamped it on the bottom too."

What starts with T, ends with T, and is full of T?

Teapot.

DOCTOR: "After the operation, you'll be a new man."

PATIENT: "Could you send the bill to the old man?"

The interviewer examined the job application, then turned to the prospective employee. "I see you have put ASAP down for the date you are available to start. However, I see you've written down AMAP for required salary. I don't believe I'm aware of what that means."

The applicant replied, "As Much As Possible!"

How did the carpenter break his teeth?

He chewed on his nails.

What training do you need to be a garbage collector?

None; you just pick things up as you go along.

Why is a bad joke like a broken pencil?

It has no point.

"I think I deserve a raise," the man said to his boss. "You know there are three other companies after me."

"Is that right?" asked the manager. "What other companies are after you?"

"The electric company, the phone company, and the gas company."

What is the longest word in the English language?

Smiles. There's a mile between the Ss.

TEACHER: Cathy, what would you do if you were being chased by a man-eating tiger?

CATHY: Nothing. I'm a girl.

What fruit is often hired by the navy?

Naval oranges.

I'm reading an incredibly interesting book about antigravity. I just can't put it down.

Why did the basketball team flood the gymnasium?

It was the only way they could sink any baskets.

Why did the amoeba flunk the math test?

Because it multiplied by dividing.

MORGAN: "My great-great-great-grandfather fought with General Washington."

MITCH: "I don't doubt it. Your family will fight with anybody."

STUDENT: "I'd like to check out this book on blood clots."

LIBRARIAN: "I'm sorry; that doesn't circulate."

What happens when a lightbulb dresses up in a suit of armor?

He becomes a knight light.

A man rode into town on Monday, stayed five days, and then rode out on Monday. How is this possible?

His horse was named Monday.

Where do hot dogs dance?

At meatballs.

A man went to the airline counter. The ticket agent asked, "Sir, do you have reservations?"

"Reservations?" he replied. "Of course I have reservations, but I'm flying anyway."

> ### The more you take away, the bigger it gets—what is it?
>
> *A hole.*

Tell a man there are three hundred billion stars in the universe, and he believes you. Tell him a bench has wet paint on it, and he has to touch it to be sure.

CARL: My upstairs neighbors are so loud. Yesterday they were banging on the floor all night.

KARL: Did they wake you?

CARL: No. Fortunately I was playing my tuba.

MANUEL: "Do you think anyone can really tell the future with cards?"

TODD: "My mom can. She took a look at my report card and told me exactly what was going to happen when my dad got home."

Why was Snow White elected to the Supreme Court?

She was the fairest of them all.

Knock-knock.
Who's there?
Pecan.
Pecan who?
Pecan someone your
own size.

Why did the cucumber need a lawyer?

It was in a pickle.

A weary traveler decided to find a hotel for the night. He stumbled to the front desk and said, "Pardon me, ma'am. I'm exhausted—I've been driving for fourteen hours, I'm hungry, and I have a headache. Can you please just tell me what room I'm in?"

"Certainly, sir," the helpful clerk replied. "You're in the lobby."

How are a lawyer and an escaped prisoner similar?

They both had to pass the bars.

CHRIS: "Uh-oh. I just made an illegal left turn."

MIKE: "That's okay. The police car behind you did the same thing."

What goes up and down but doesn't move?

A staircase.

HEARD ANOTHER GREAT JOKE? WRITE IT HERE!

HA HA HA
HA

....
....
....
....
....
....
....
....
....
....

What did the judge say to his dentist?

"Pull my tooth, the whole tooth, and nothing but the tooth."

A man was on a business trip and asked the hotel clerk for a restaurant she might recommend.

"There's a good place across the street that says it can serve anything a customer orders," she said.

The man headed over for dinner, and after considering the menu, ordered baked armadillo and biscuits.

"I'm sorry, sir, you'll have to order something else," the waitress said. "We're all out of biscuits."

Why was the cat afraid of the tree?
He didn't like its bark.

"I don't believe for a second that weightlifting is a sport," Chuck said. "They pick up a heavy thing and put it down again. I call that indecision."

A man took his Rottweiler to the vet and said to him, "My dog is cross-eyed. Is there anything you can do for it?"

"Well," said the vet, "let me take a look at him." So he picked up the dog and had a good look at its eyes.

"Well," said the vet, "I'm going to have to put him down."

"Just because he's cross-eyed?" asked the man.

"No," said the vet, "because he's heavy."

What do cats drink on hot summer afternoons?

Mice tea.

BILL: Why are you dating Melanie?

WILL: Because she's different than other girls.

BILL: How so?

WILL: She's the only one who'll go out with me.

A couple was going out for the evening to celebrate their anniversary. While they were getting ready, the husband put the cat outside. The taxi arrived, and as the couple walked out the door, the cat shot back into the house.

Not wanting their pet to have free run of the house while they were out, the husband went back upstairs to get the cat.

The wife didn't want it known that there would be no one home, so she said to the taxi driver, "My husband will be right back. He's just going upstairs to say goodbye to his mother."

A few minutes later, the husband climbed into the car and said, "I'm sorry I took so long. The old thing was hiding under the bed, so I had to poke her with a coat hanger to get her to come out!"

How do poets take their wedding vows?

For better or verse.

FIRST ALIEN: Is there somewhere I can go to get cleaned up?

SECOND ALIEN: Yup. Go straight and you'll come to the meteor showers.

What makes a road bread?

The letter b.

A tour guide was showing a tourist around Washington, DC. The guide pointed out the place where George Washington supposedly threw a dollar across the Potomac River.

"That's impossible," said the tourist. "No one could throw a coin that far!"

"Well, remember," replied the guide. "A dollar went a lot farther in those days."

A couple went on a safari deep in Africa. They were walking through the jungle when a lion jumped out in front of them and grabbed the wife in its jaws.

"Shoot!" screamed the woman. "Shoot!"

"I can't!" her husband hollered back. "The battery in the camera is dead!"

What are geese bumps for?

To keep geese from speeding.

"Did I ever tell you about my adventures eradicating alligators from the streets of Manhattan?"

"There are no alligators on the streets of Manhattan."

"Nope. Not anymore."

What does the sun drink out of?

Sunglasses.

"You must be the worst caddie in the world," said the dejected golfer after a disastrous afternoon on the course.

"I doubt it, sir," replied the caddie. "That would be too much of a coincidence."

BOY: Dad, which do you think is America's worst problem: ignorance or apathy?

DAD: Don't know. Don't really care, either.

When is a bicycle not a bicycle?

When it turns into a driveway.

Two friends were discussing the relative merits of car models.

"I'm waiting for a car that'll last me a life-time," said one.

"I hope to live longer than that," said the other.

BERT: "Why do you keep singing the same song over and over?"

GERT: "The melody haunts me."

BERT: "That's because you're murdering it!"

What goes tick–tick woof–woof?

A watchdog.

HARRY: Hey, Larry! Nice trumpet you've got there.

LARRY: I borrowed it from my neighbor.

HARRY: I didn't know you played the trumpet.

LARRY: I can't. And now, neither can my neighbor.

Never marry a tennis player.

To her, love means nothing.

HEARD ANOTHER GREAT JOKE? WRITE IT HERE!

....

....

....

....

....

....

....

....

How many psychiatrists does it take to change a light bulb?

One, but only if the light bulb wants to change.

Why do bees hum?

Because they can't remember the words.

Where do wardens take the criminally insane for a walk?

Along the psycho-path.

How did the solar system hold up its pants?

With an asteroid belt.

"Are caterpillars good to eat?" asked a little boy at the dinner table.

"No," said his father. "Why would you ask a question like that?"

"Well, there was one in your salad, but it's gone now."

Necessity is the mother of invention—even though much of what's invented is hardly necessary.

> **What sits on the bottom of the ocean and twitches?**
>
> *A nervous wreck.*

JUNE: Will February March?

JAN: No, but April May.

> **What stays in the corner but travels far?**
>
> *A stamp.*

TOM: "What is the first thing you lose on a diet?"

DOT: "Your patience."

CELEBRITY: "It is so good to be with you wonderful people here at Shady Rest Nursing Home. Does anyone here know who I am?"

RESIDENT: "No, but don't worry. If you go down to the front desk, they'll tell you."

"Halloween was confusing," said little Georgie. "All my life my parents said, 'Never take candy from strangers.' And then they dressed me up in a costume and said, 'Go ask for candy.'"

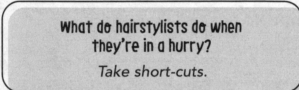

What do hairstylists do when they're in a hurry?

Take short-cuts.

PASSENGER: Can I take this train to New York?

CONDUCTOR: No, sir, it's much too heavy for you.

What kind of running means
you will have to walk?

Running out of gas.

Knock-knock.
Who's there?
Honey hive.
Honey hive who?
Honey, hive got a
crush on you.

Why did the star get arrested?

Because it was a shooting star.

PATIENT: "Nurse, nurse!"

NURSE: "What is it, sir?"

PATIENT: "I keep seeing spots in front of my eyes."

NURSE: "Have you seen a doctor?"

PATIENT: "No, just spots."

TEACHER: "How long did the Hundred Years' War last?"

STUDENT: "I don't know. Ten years?"

TEACHER: "No! Think carefully. How old is a five-year-old horse?"

STUDENT, THOUGHTFULLY: "Oh, five years old!"

TEACHER: "That's right. So how long did the Hundred Years' War last?"

STUDENT: "Now I get it—five years!"

What kind of bird does construction work?

The crane.

A rule was posted in large letters in the school hallway: SHOES REQUIRED IN THE CAFETERIA. In the margin, someone had scribbled: SOCKS MUST GO TO THE GYM.

A police officer saw a woman sitting in her car with a tiger in the front seat next to her. The officer said, "It's against the law to have that tiger in your car. Take him to the zoo." The next day the police officer saw the same woman in the same car with the same tiger. He said, "I told you yesterday to take that tiger to the zoo!" The woman replied, "I did. He had such a good time, today we're going to the beach!"

Why did the alien threw beef on the asteroid?

He wanted it a little meteor.

Knock-knock.
Who's there?
Dishes.
Dishes who?
Dishes the police.
Open the door.

One astronaut asks another astronaut if he has ever heard of the planet Saturn. The second astronaut says, "I'm not sure, but it has a familiar ring."

What do you get from a pampered cow?

Spoiled milk.

There's a good reason some people can't seem to mind their own business. Usually, it's because they have either (1) no mind or (2) no business.

What do math teachers like to eat with their coffee?

A slice of pi.

What dog can jump higher than a tree?

Any dog can jump higher than a tree. Trees don't jump.

DOCTOR: "I'm afraid you have a dangerously advanced case of bronchitis."

PATIENT: "I only had the sniffles when I first sat down in your waiting room."

Why was the rabbit so unhappy?

She was having a bad hare day.

Did you hear about the new restaurant that just opened on the moon?

Good food, but no atmosphere.

What's a good name for a lawyer?

Sue.

It's always better to say nothing and have people wonder about your intelligence than to say something stupid and leave them no doubt.

HEARD ANOTHER GREAT JOKE? WRITE IT HERE!

HA HA HA
HA

....
....
....
....
....
....
....
....
....

What do you call something that everyone asks for, everyone gives, everyone needs, but very few people take?

Advice.

Some teenaged friends were marveling at the scene of an accident where one of them miraculously had walked away from the mishap without a scratch the night before.

"Wow, that was some smashup," said one.

"Totaled the car," said another.

"How'd it happen?" asked a third.

The victim pointed to a tilted telephone pole. "See that?"

"Yeah."

"I didn't."

What do you get when you buy a boat at a discount?

A sale-boat.

What happened to the wooden car with wooden wheels and a wooden engine?

It wooden go.

What did the tornado say to the sports car?
"Let's go for a spin!"

> **Who earns a living by driving their customers away?**
>
> *A taxi driver.*

What's a light-year?
The same as a regular year but with less calories.

> **How do you know when the moon is going broke?**
>
> *When it's down to its last quarter.*

The boss called one of his employees into the office. "Rob," he said, "you've been with the company for six months. You started off in the mailroom. Just one week later, you were promoted to a sales position, and one month after that you were promoted to district sales manager. Just four months later, you were promoted to vice president. Now it's time for me to retire, and I want you to take over the company. What do you say to that?"

"Thanks," said the employee.

"Thanks?" the boss replied. "That's all you can say?"

"Oh, sorry," the employee said. "Thanks, Dad."

A woman stepped up to a travel desk and asked for a roundtrip ticket. "Where to?" asked the agent. The woman looked offended. "Right back here. Where do you think?"

> ## What's a history teacher's favorite quiz show?
> *The Dating Game.*

DOCTOR: "How is the boy who swallowed the quarter?"

NURSE: "No change yet."

> ## Where do you take a sick puppy?
> *To the dogtor.*

SON: "Dad, what's middle age?"

FATHER: "That's when you lose all your growth at the top and do all your growing in the middle."

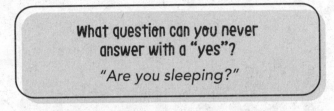

What question can you never answer with a "yes"?

"Are you sleeping?"

TEACHER: "Class, are you looking forward to our field trip to the national tree museum?"

STUDENT: "Well, I could take it or leaf it."

What goes from Maine to Florida without moving?

The highway

> **What rock group has four members, all of whom are dead, one of whom was assassinated?**
>
> *Mount Rushmore.*

A man was visiting a college. He paused to admire the new Hemingway Hall that had recently been constructed on campus. "It's marvelous to see a building named for Ernest Hemingway," he said.

"Actually," said the guide, "it's named for William Hemingway. No relation."

The visitor was astonished. "Was William Hemingway a writer too?" he asked.

"Oh, yes," said his guide. "He wrote the check."

> **What kind of ant is good at math?**
>
> *An account-ant.*

Knock-knock.
Who's there?
Boo!
Boo, who?
Well, you don't have
to cry about it!

Did you hear the story about the peacock that crossed the road?

It is really a colorful tail. . . .

A little boy went to the pet shop to buy a new food dish for his dog. "Would you like to have your dog's name on the bowl?" the clerk asked.

"No, thanks. She can't read."

What can fall but will never break, and what can break but will never fall?

Night and day.

HEARD ANOTHER GREAT JOKE? WRITE IT HERE!

HA HA HA
HA

....

....

....

....

....

....

....

....

When full, I can point the way, but when empty, nothing moves me. I have two skins—one outside and one inside. What am I?

A glove.

A patrol officer chased down a speeder after a thirty-mile adventure on the interstate—only after the speeder had run out of gas. "Congratulations," said the officer sarcastically. "You hit 163 miles per hour. I didn't think a little subcompact like that could give me such a run."

"And congratulations to you. I didn't think you could keep up."

What kind of lights did Noah have on the ark?

Floodlights.

What did the lovesick bull say to the cow? "When I fall in love, it will be for heifer."

How can the statement "Four is half of five" be true?

If four is written in roman numerals (IV), then it is half of F(IV)E.

What's an astronaut's favorite sandwich?

Launch meat.

A tenth-grade boy came home with a poor report card. As he handed it to his father, he asked, "What do you think is wrong, Dad, my heredity or my environment?"

What bone will a dog never eat?

A trombone.

Why was the sailor afraid of geometry?

He heard the Bermuda Triangle will make you disappear.

Why did the army begin drafting babies?

It was trying to build up the infantry.

"When did Adam and Eve eat the apple?" a Sunday school teacher asked.

"In the summertime," answered a student.

"Why, Brenda, how do you know that?" the teacher asked.

"Well, we all know it was just before the fall."

If King Henry VIII were alive today, what would he be most famous for?

Extreme old age.

Knock-knock.
Who's there?
Aardvark.
Aardvark who?
"Aardvark a million miles to be with you."

"I really appreciate your coming out to our house this late at night," remarked a sick patient.

"No problem," said the doctor. "I had to come see Mr. Oaks just down the road, anyway. This way I can kill two birds with one stone."

When is the best time to make a dentist appointment?

Tooth-hurty.

ELLA: "I just adore tennis. I could play like this forever."

MARK: "You will, if you don't take lessons."

Why is the law of gravity untrustworthy?

It will always let you down.

What happens when two ropes get into a contest?

They always tie.

What did King George say when he heard about the rebellious American colonies?

"How revolting!"

A fisherman was bragging about a monster of a fish he caught. A friend broke in and chided, "Yeah, I saw a picture of that fish, and he was all of six inches long."

"Yeah," said the proud fisherman. "But after battling for three hours, a fish can lose a lot of weight."

Knock-knock.
Who's there?
Spell.
Spell who?
W-H-O!

> **What numbers are always wandering around?**
>
> *Roamin' numerals*

At night they come without being called And move around without being walled. But at the very first sign of light, they disappear back into the night. What are they?
Stars.

> **Why was 6 afraid of 7?**
>
> *Because 7, 8, 9.*

How many legs does a horse have?
Six. It has forelegs in the front and two legs in the back.

"I think the older my grandpa gets," a girl remarked to a friend, "the farther he had to walk to school when he was my age."

Where do you go to school to learn how to greet people?

Hi school.

A carpenter fell two stories and landed with a thud on his back. "What happened?" asked a coworker, rushing to his side.

"I'm not sure," the victim said. "I just got here."

Which teacher always uses words twice?

A history teacher, because history always repeats itself.

Why did the teacher marry the school janitor?
Because he swept her off her feet!

Traveling through New England, a motorist stopped for gas in a small town. "What is this town called?" he asked the station attendant.

"That all depends," replied the man. "Do you mean by them that has to live in this secluded place, or by them that's merely enjoying its quaint and picturesque rustic charm for a short spell?"

What do you get when you cross a Dalmatian with a fountain pen?

Ink spots.

Buyer: Hey, you told me you had purebred police dogs for sale. This animal is the mangiest, dirtiest, scrawniest mutt I've ever laid eyes on. How can you get away with calling him a police dog.

Breeder: He works undercover.

Why did the star athlete never listen to music?

She always broke the record.

HEARD ANOTHER GREAT JOKE? WRITE IT HERE!

HA HA HA HA

A woman wrote a check at a department store. "I'll have to ask you to identify yourself," the clerk said.

The customer took a small mirror from her handbag, looked into it keenly and pronounced, "Yes. That's definitely me."

Why did the teacher have
to turn the lights on?

Because her class was so dim.

Why was there thunder and lightning in the chemistry lab?

Because the scientists were brainstorming.

Why did the poor dog chase his own tail?

He was trying to make both ends meet.

Little Henry got a violin and played it night and day. Unfortunately, every time he played a note, the family dog would whine and howl endlessly.

One afternoon, unable to stand the dog's suffering any longer, Henry's little sister stormed into his room and begged, "For goodness' sake! Can't you please play something the dog doesn't know?"

An elderly couple had finally saved enough money for a trip around the world. They had never flown on a plane before and were eager to experience air travel.

As they arrived in Chicago, they rolled to a stop, and a little red truck drove up and refueled the plane.

They next landed in Seattle, and again, a red truck pulled up to refuel the plane.

"These planes make great time, don't they, dear?" asked the husband.

"Yes, they do," replied the wife. "And that little red truck doesn't do too bad, either!"

What do you do if a teacher rolls her eyes at you?

Pick them up and roll them back to her.

When is a baby good at basketball?
When it's dribbling.

Mrs. Chapman spotted a weight machine as she was walking through the airport. She was curious about the machine, so she deposited a quarter and stepped onto it. A computerized voice stated, "You are five feet, six inches tall, weigh 160 pounds, and you are taking a plane to London."

She was impressed with the accuracy of the machine and decided to try it again. "You are five feet, six inches tall, weigh 160 pounds, and you are taking a plane to London," said the voice.

Mrs. Chapman wanted to try once more, but this time she decided to fool it. She went into the ladies' room, changed her sweater, and put on a hat. She returned and dropped another quarter into the slot. The voice came again, "You are five feet, six inches tall, weigh 160 pounds," and added, "and while you were in the ladies' room, you missed the plane to London."

Why can't you ever trust atoms?

They make up everything.

What do you call a poodle in a sauna?
A hot dog.

What bites without any teeth?

Frost.

What did the dog get when he multiplied 413 by 782?
The wrong answer.

What's an infant's favorite plant?

Baby's breath.

What is the one thing you can always count on?
Your fingers.

If one synchronized swimmer drowns, do the rest have to drown too?

> **What's the best thing to take on a trip to the desert?**
>
> *A thirst-aid kit.*

Coming home from his Little League game, Bud burst through the front door.

His father immediately asked, "So how did you do, son?"

"You'll never believe it!" Buddy announced. "I was responsible for the winning run!"

"Really? How'd you do that?"

"I dropped the ball."

> **What do you give a mummy for Christmas?**
>
> *Wrapping paper.*

What did the flower say to the bee?
"Quit bugging me!"

A famous art collector was strolling through the city when he noticed a mangy cat drinking milk from a saucer in the doorway of a store.

He did a double take, as he observed that the saucer was quite rare and very valuable. He walked casually into the store and offered to buy the cat for two dollars. The store owner replied, "I'm sorry, but the cat is not for sale."

The collector persisted, saying, "Please, I need a hungry cat around the house to catch mice. I'll pay you twenty-five dollars for the cat."

The owner said, "Sold," and handed over the cat.

The collector continued, "For the twenty-five dollars, could you throw in the saucer too? I'm sure the cat is used to it, and I won't have to purchase a dish for her."

The owner replied, "Sorry, Pal, but that is my lucky saucer. So far this week I've sold fifty-nine cats."

Which vegetable wasn't allowed on Christopher Columbus's ships?

The leek.

What was the colonist's favorite drink?

Liber-tea.

The owner of a small deli was audited by IRS. He had reported a net profit of $70,000 for the year.

"I work hard for my money," the deli owner said. "My family helps out, and the deli is only closed three days a year. And you're asking how I made $70,000?"

"Oh, it isn't your income that's the problem," the tax agent said. "It's the deductions. You listed five trips to the Bahamas for you and your wife."

"Oh, that," the owner said with a smile. "Apparently you didn't know—we deliver."

What kind of bow is impossible to tie?

A rainbow.

HEARD ANOTHER GREAT JOKE? WRITE IT HERE!

HA HA HA HA

....

....

....

....

....

....

....

....

....

TEACHER: "Can anyone tell me why the Capitol in Washington has a rotunda?"

STUDENT: "So our politicians can run around in circles?"

Why is Alabama the smartest state in the United States?

Because it has four As and one B.

Why did the skeleton go
to the party alone?

It had no body to go with.

A pharmacist was squinting and holding the prescription slip up to the light. Finally she took up a magnifier in a futile effort to read it.

"We don't think too highly of this particular doctor," she told the customer, "but there's one thing he obviously can do better than anyone else on the planet."

"What's that?"

"Read his own handwriting."

Which animals were hardest
for Noah to trust?

The cheetahs.

A man went to his doctor and told him that he hadn't been feeling well lately. The doctor examined the man, left the room and came back with three different bottles of pills.

"Take the green pill with a big glass of water when you wake up," he said. "Take the blue pill with a big glass of water after you eat lunch. Then just before going to bed take the red pill with another big glass of water."

Startled to be put on so much medicine the man said, "Oh, Doc! Now you got me worried! Exactly what is my problem?"

The doctor replied, "You're not drinking enough water."

What belongs to you but other people use most often?

Your name.

SHIRLEY: "I weighed only two pounds when I was born."

ELLEN: "Wow! Did you survive?"

Ben took Lisa, his girlfriend, to her first football game. Afterwards, he asked her how she liked the game.

"I liked it, but I couldn't understand why they were killing each other for twenty-five cents," she asked.

"What do you mean?"

"Well, everyone kept yelling, 'Get the quarter back!'"

What do you call a cow eating grass in your yard?

A lawn moo-er.

Mort is in his usual place at the breakfast table, reading the morning paper. He comes across an article about a beautiful actress who was about to marry a football player known for his lack of general intelligence.

He turns to his wife and blurts, "I'll never understand why the biggest dummies get the most attractive wives."

His wife replies, "Why, thank you, dear!"

Four men were playing a round of golf. "These hills are getting steeper as the years go by," one complained.

"The sand traps seem to be bigger than I remember them too," said another senior.

After hearing enough, the oldest and wisest of the four, at eighty-seven, said, "Just be thankful we're still on the right side of the grass!"

What is the moon worth?

Four quarters.

MIKE: "I heard you got kicked out of the zoo last week."

IKE: "Yeah, for feeding the squirrels."

MIKE: "Wow, I know they don't like for people to feed the animals, but that seems like strong punishment."

IKE: "Actually, I was feeding the squirrels to the cougars."

A pet shop owner was trying to talk Mrs. McLellan into buying a dog for her children. "Oh, they'll love this little rascal!" said the clerk. "He's full of fun and he eats anything. He especially likes children."

What disease do chickens dread the worst?

People pox.

One morning, as a man prepares to leave town, he stops by his office to pick up messages. While at the office, the night watchman stops in and says, "Sir, don't go on this trip. I had a dream last night that the plane will crash and you will die!" So the man decides to cancel his trip.

Just as the watchman predicted, the plane crashes and no one survives. The very next morning, the man rewards the watchman with a thousand dollars, then fires him. Why?

The night watchman had been sleeping on the job!

A salesman entered a yard and saw two little girls playing with a dog. "Does your dog bite?" he asked the children.

"Oh, no, sir. Our dog has never bitten anyone."

The salesman then walked up the steps to ring the doorbell for the parents. Suddenly, the dog jumped on the porch and bit him fiercely on the leg.

"Hey, you said your dog doesn't bite!" the salesman yelled at the girls.

"Our dog doesn't. That's somebody else's dog."

What kind of vegetable do you find under elephants' feet?

Squash.

MRS. LAIRD: "Do you ever wake up grouchy in the morning?"

MRS. BAIRD: "No, I usually let him just get up whenever he's ready."

What did Natasha do when she found her pet dog eating her dictionary?

She took the words right out of his mouth.

What kind of cheese did Frankenstein like?

Muenster.

Dr. James wasn't at all pleased to discover Mrs. Bryan had come to him for a third opinion before agreeing to surgery. "You should have come to me to begin with," he stated. "Who did you see first?"

"Dr. Morgan."

"Well, I suppose there are worse doctors, but the man has no vision. What did he tell you?"

"He said I need surgery, but I should get another doctor's opinion."

"And who did you see next?"

"Dr. Lattimore."

"That dummy! His knowledge of medicine could be contained in a thimble. His advice is totally worthless. What on earth did he tell you?"

"He told me to come see you."

Enormous: a very large moose

> **How did the boat show affection?**
>
> *It hugged the shore.*

"What's your dog's name?"

"Ginger, when she's not biting people."

"What's her name when she is biting people?"

"Ginger Snaps."

> **What do you call a snake who gets elected mayor?**
>
> *A civil serpent.*

"Do you think Dottie's clean?" asked Myra, bringing her Dalmatian to show Mom after bathing the dog.

"Yes," Mom said, inspecting the ears and paws. "She's pretty clean."

"Actually," said Myra, "I think she's pretty even when she's dirty."

HEARD ANOTHER GREAT JOKE? WRITE IT HERE!

HA
HA HA
HA

....
....
....
....
....
....
....
....
....

I come in different shapes and sizes. Part of me has curves; part of me is straight. You can put me anywhere you like, but there is only one right place for me. What am I?

A jigsaw puzzle.

A little boy was overheard talking to himself as he strutted through his backyard, carrying a ball and bat and shouting, "I'm the greatest hitter in the world!" Then he tossed the ball into the air, swung at it, and missed. "Strike one!" he yelled.

Undaunted, he picked up the ball and repeated, "I'm the greatest hitter in the world!" When it came down, he swung again and missed. "Strike two!" he cried.

The boy paused a moment, examined the ball, spit on his hands, adjusted his hat, and repeated, "I'm the greatest hitter in the world!" Again he tossed the ball up and swung at it. He missed. "Strike three!"

"Wow!" he exclaimed. "I'm the greatest pitcher in the world!"

What should you do if you find a five-hundred-pound dog asleep on your bed?

Sleep on the sofa.

Why are pianos difficult to get into?
The keys are on the inside.

In a small town the veterinarian, who was also the chief of police, was awakened by the telephone.

"Please hurry!" said the woman's voice on the other end of the line.

"Do you need the police or a vet?" he asked.

"Both," the woman replied. "I'm not able to get my dog's mouth open, and there's a burglar's leg in it."

How do you catch a school of fish?

With a bookworm.

Do you say, "Eight and four is eleven" or "Eight and four are eleven"?

Neither. Eight and four are twelve.

WILLIAM: "I can stop a charging elephant with one hand."

PETE: "I don't believe an elephant with one hand would be charging."

How did the Vikings send secret messages?

By Norse code.

Mom and Dad were getting started with Saturday chores when their child came out into the yard. "Why don't you go across the street and ask how old Mrs. Wells is this morning?" Dad suggested. The child dutifully crossed the street, greeted their neighbor three doors down, and asked the question, "Dad wants to know how old you are this morning." Back home, the child reported to his parents, "Mrs. Wells said to tell you to mind your own business."

What did the fish boat captain say to the card magician?

"Pick a cod, any cod."

An accountant is having a hard time sleeping and goes to see his doctor. "Doctor, I just can't get to sleep at night."

"Have you tried counting sheep?"

"That's the problem. I make a mistake and then spend three hours trying to find it."

What do you call a nine-foot high stack of frogs?

A toadem pole.

"It's obvious," said the teacher, "that you haven't studied your geography. What is your excuse?"

"Well," the student replied, "my dad says the world is changing every day, so I thought it would be best if I waited until it settles down."

Why do people with colds feel so tired?

Their noses are always running.

Knock-knock.
Who's there?
Waddle.
Waddle who?
Waddle you give
me if I stop telling
these jokes?

What's the best way to clear frogs off your car windows?

With the defrogger.

Why do giraffes have such small appetites?
Because with them, a little goes a long way.

What's the favorite city of hamsters?

Hamsterdam.

Eggs and ham: A day's work for a chicken, a lifetime commitment for a pig.

What force and strength cannot break through, I with barely a touch can do. And many in the street would wait, Were I not a friend to the gate. What am I?

A key.

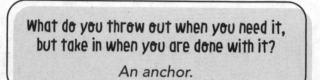

What do you throw out when you need it, but take in when you are done with it?

An anchor.

"Look over there!" said the frightened skunk to his pal. "There's a human with a gun, and he's getting closer and closer! What are we going to do?"

The second skunk bowed his head and calmly replied, "Let us spray."

"How's your sick horse?" one rancher asked another.

"She's in stable condition."

A traveler was visiting Sydney, Australia. He pulled up at a bus stop where two locals were standing. "Entschuldigung, koennen Sie Deutsch sprechen?" he asked.

The two stared at him.

"Excusez-moi, parlez-vous français?" he tried.

The two continue to stare.

"Parlare italiano?"

No response.

"Hablan ustedes español?"

Still no reply.

The driver sped off, disgusted. The first man turned to the second one and said, "You know, maybe we should learn a foreign language."

"Why?" asked the other. "That guy knew four languages, and it didn't do him any good, did it?"

Which side of a horse usually has the most hair?

The outside.

IDA: "What's orange and has green spots, eight legs and one red eye?"

ERMA: "I give up. What?"

IDA: "I don't know, but there's one crawling up your back."

"I didn't see you in any of our classes yesterday," said Kimberly. "You must've missed school."

"Not much," said Kenny.

\What kind of can never needs a can opener?

A pelican.

A boy was at a carnival and went to a booth where a man said to the boy, "If I write your exact weight on this piece of paper, then you have to give me fifty dollars; but if I can't, I will pay you fifty dollars." The boy looked around and saw no scale, so he agreed, thinking no matter what the man wrote he'd just say he weighed more or less. In the end the boy ended up paying the man fifty dollars. How did the man win the bet?

The man wrote, "Your exact weight," on the paper.

What kind of insect marries a ladybug?

A gentlemanbug.

"We have a real problem with biting insects around our yard," a customer told a pharmacist. "What can we do about it?"

"Stop biting them," said the pharmacist.

How do you fix a broken chimp?

With a monkey wrench.

"How much money do you think I'm worth, Dad?"

The father regarded his teenaged son thoughtfully. "To your mother and me, I would say you're priceless."

"Do you think I'm worth a thousand dollars?"

"Certainly."

"A million?"

"Even more than a million, to us."

"Would you mind giving me about twenty of it, then?"

What do you call mouse shoes?

Squeakers.

Some Boy Scouts from the city were on a camping trip. The mosquitoes were so fierce, the boys had to hide under their blankets to avoid being bitten. Then one of the scouts saw some lightning bugs and said to his friend, "We might as well give up. They're coming after us with flashlights."

How does an octopus go into battle?

Fully armed.

WOMAN: "My husband snores so loudly he keeps everybody in the house awake. What can we do?"

DOCTOR: "Try turning him on his side, massaging his shoulders and neck, and stuffing a washcloth into his mouth."

How do pigs say goodbye?

With hogs and kisses.

My cat is so smart. He eats cheese, then waits at the mouse hole with baited breath.

> **What grows up while it grows down?**
> *A baby duckling*

Why did the farmer raise his children in a barn?

He wanted them to grow up in a stable environment.

> **How can you tell if a tree is a dogwood?**
> *By its bark.*

A man walked into a church, looking for a place to sit. Spying an empty seat, he asked the woman sitting beside it, "Is that seat next to you saved?"

"No," she replied, "but I'm praying for it."

"Have you got any kittens going cheap?" asked a customer in a pet shop.

"No, sir," replied the owner. "All our kittens go, 'Meow.'"

What do you call a time–out
in the Lions' football game?

A paws

A cowboy had two horses, but he couldn't tell them apart. He cut off one horse's mane, but it grew back; he cut off the tail, but that grew back too. A friend suggested that he measure the horses. The cowboy measured them and went to his friend and said, "That was a great idea—the black one was two inches taller than the white one."

How do you make a skunk stop smelling?
Pinch its nose.

What does an educated owl say?
Whom.

How do you make an elephant float?
Start with your favorite ice cream, pour in some root beer, and add elephant.

What's the difference between an elephant in Africa and an elephant in India?
Several thousand miles.

STEVE: "How did your parakeet die?"

FRED: "Flu."

STEVE: "Don't be silly. Parakeets don't die from the flu."

FRED: "Mine did. He flew under a bus."

DENNIS: "Steve's changed his mind again."

SUZANNE: "Well, I hope this one's got more sense than the last one he had."

> **What did the pea patch say to the corn patch?**
>
> *Stop stalking me.*

DEE DEE: "Did you know Santa Claus has a secret fear of crawling down chimneys?"

PEE WEE: "No! Is he afraid of closed-in places?"

DEE DEE: "Yes. It's a condition called Claustrophobia."

Several security guards were scratching their heads in the aftermath of a bank robbery.

"But how could they have gotten away?" one wondered aloud. "We had all the exits guarded."

"I think they must have gone out the entrance," suggested another.

> ### How do you catch a unique rabbit?
> *Unique up on it.*

What do you call a dog with a cold?
A germy shepherd.

INGRID: "Do you know what makes the Tower of Pisa lean?"
PETER: "It's malnourished, I guess."

A chicken walks into a restaurant. The hostess says, "We don't serve poultry!"
The chicken says, "That's okay; I just want a soda."

HEARD ANOTHER GREAT JOKE? WRITE IT HERE!

HA HA HA HA

....

....

....

....

....

....

....

....

....

A prospector straggled into town, went into the little cafe and told the owner, "Buddy, I'm starved almost to death. It's been two weeks since I've tasted food." The bartender responded, "Well, it all tastes about the same as it did back then."

One day a chicken went to a library and said, "Book, book, book." The librarian gave the chicken three books, and the chicken went on its way. The next day the same chicken came into the library and said, "Book, book, book." So the librarian gave the chicken three books again, but this time she became suspicious of where the chicken was taking the books, so she decided to follow the chicken. After awhile, the chicken came to a swamp and stopped beside a frog. The chicken gave the three books to the frog, and the frog said, "Read it! Read it! Read it!"

> **What is a shark's favorite game?**
> *Swallow the leader.*

SUSAN: "We have a terrible problem. Our mother thinks she's a chicken."

WANDA: "Why don't you take her to a psychiatrist?"

SUSAN: "We need the eggs."

> **Where do sheep go on vacation?**
>
> *To the Baahamas.*

A poor bookseller walked through Central Park on his way home each evening. One Monday a masked man jumped from behind a tree. "Give me your money!"

"I have no money. I'm just a poor bookseller. Here's my wallet; see for yourself."

Finding the wallet and the victim's pockets all empty, the bandit grumbled and ran off into the darkening shrubbery.

The next Monday the same bandit accosted the bookseller. "Give me your money!" Again he made off without a dime.

This happened each Monday evening for a month. Finally the bookseller said to him, "Look, you recognize me. You know I'm only a poor bookseller, and I don't carry any money at all. Why do you waste your time and risk getting caught every Monday?"

The robber replied, "I'm still practicing, and you don't seem to mind too much."

Two guys were hiking in the forest when they suddenly came across a big grizzly bear. The one guy took off his hiking boots and put on some running shoes. His friend said to him, "You're crazy! Don't you know how fast grizzlies are? You'll never be able to outrun it!"

"Outrun it?" said his friend. "I only have to outrun you!"

What is the hardest thing about learning to skate?

The ice.

Frustrated dragon on the field of battle: "Mother always said there would be knights like this."

What kind of snake is good at math?

An adder.

What is the difference between a teacher and a railway engineer?

One trains the mind and the other minds the train.

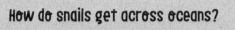

How do snails get across oceans?

In snailboats.

Why did the woman tiptoe past her medicine cabinet?

She didn't want to wake the sleeping pills.

When is fishing not a good way to relax?

When you're the worm.

ERSKINE: "I think I need to clean my tuba."

BAND DIRECTOR: "Try this tuba toothpaste."

SALLY: "My mother has trained herself to walk in her sleep every night."

CAL: "Why would she want to do that?"

SALLY: "To save time. This way she can get her exercise and her rest all at once."

Have you heard about the dog that ate an onion?

Its bark was much worse than its bite.

"Do you think the skunk would be considered a very popular animal?" the teacher asked.

"Not exactly— but it's always the scenter of attention," the student answered.

MOTHER: "Troy, I've been calling you for the last five minutes! Didn't you hear me?"

TROY: "No, I didn't hear you until the fourth time you called."

What bird is always out of breath?

A puffin.

At the end of his shift, the police officer parked his police van in front of the station. His K-9 partner, Bo, was in the back. As the officer was exiting his car, a little boy walked by and looked in the back window of the van. "Is that a dog you got back there?" the boy asked.

"It sure is," the officer replied.

Puzzled, the boy looked at the officer, then back at the van. Finally he said, "What did he do?"

Commentator: an everyday potato.

The farmer's son was returning from the market with a crate of chickens his father had entrusted to him, when all of a sudden the box fell and broke open. Chickens scurried off in different directions, but the boy jogged all over the neighborhood, retrieving the birds and returning them to the repaired crate.

Hoping he had found them all, the boy went home. "Pa, the chickens got loose," he told his father reluctantly, "but I managed to find all nine of them."

"You did well, son," the farmer said, "because you left with only six."

Does a leopard change its spots?

*When it's tired of one spot,
it just moves to another.*

What animal makes it hard to carry on a conversation?

A goat, because he always wants to butt in.

HEARD ANOTHER GREAT JOKE? WRITE IT HERE!

....

....

....

....

....

....

....

....

....

MUSIC TEACHER: In the basic choir, there are two male vocal parts. One is the tenor. What is the other?

STUDENT: Uh. . .the niner?

What did one horse say to the other horse?

"Your pace is familiar, but I don't remember your mane."

What wears a coat in the winter and pants all summer?

A dog.

The door to the Pony Express office swung open. A cowboy sprinted out, took a running leap, and landed in the middle of the road. "What's the matter with you, pardner?" asked a bystander. "Did they throw you out, or are you just crazy?"

"Neither," replied the cowboy. "But just wait until I find out who moved my horse!"

What is the best advice you can give to a worm?

"Sleep late!"

A man went to pick up his friend from the train station. When the friend got off the train, the man noticed that he was looking rather pale. "You look like you don't feel well," said the man.

"No, I always get sick when I ride backward on a train," replied the friend.

"Why didn't you ask the person across from you to change seats?" asked the man.

"Well, I thought about it," said the friend. "But there wasn't anyone there."

What kind of insects live on the moon?

Lunarticks.

A man ran up to a farmhouse and pounded on the door. When the farmer came to the door, the man demanded, "Where's the nearest train station, and what time is the next train to the city?" The farmer replied, "You may cut through my field, and you should reach the station in time for the 5:20. But if my bull sees you, you'll probably make it by 5:00."

"Your horse is very well behaved," the lady noted to the resting rider.

"Oh, that's true," he replied. "When we come to a fence, he always stops quickly and lets me go over first!"

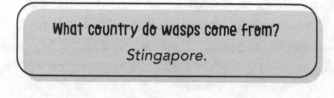

What country do wasps come from?

Stingapore.

MICHAEL: "Why are you making faces at my dog? That's silly."

ARTIE: "Well, he started it."

Why shouldn't you tell a pig a secret?

Because he's a squealer.

Cartoon: a song about an automobile.

A pair of zebras were wandering in Africa when they heard the thunderous sound of hooves over the horizon. A massive herd of giraffes appeared, running their way in a blinding cloud of dust. The zebras took cover behind a tree and waited for the giraffes to pass. Then they continued wandering.

A few hours later, another large herd of giraffes approached, stirring up a storm of dust. Again, the zebras got out of the way.

Near sundown, they found themselves in the path of a third mob of giraffes. Standing behind a rock, coughing from the thick dust as the tall animals rushed past, one zebra turned to the other and said, "I think we should move away. There's too much giraffic around here to suit me."

What do you get when you cross a hen with a hyena?

An animal that laughs at every yolk.

Where does a dog go when he loses his tail?
To the re-tailer.

Everyone knows that an elephant never forgets—but then, what does he really have to remember?

> **What do you get when you cross a pig and a tree?**
>
> *A porky pine.*

When his printing ink began to grow faint, a man called a local repair shop. The friendly salesperson who answered the phone said the printer would probably only need to be cleaned. Because the store charged fifty dollars for the cleaning, he advised the caller that he might be better off reading the printer's manual and trying to clean the machine himself. Pleasantly surprised by his candor, the caller asked, "I don't think your boss would like that you're discouraging business, would he?"

"It's actually my boss's idea," the employee admitted. "He says we usually make more money on repairs if we let people try to fix their equipment first."

> ### What is cowhide most used for?
> *Holding cows together.*

SALESMAN: You make a small down payment, but then you don't make any payments for six months.

CUSTOMER: Who told you about me?

> ### What do you call a penguin in the desert?
> *Lost.*

The manager is reviewing a potential employee's application and notes that the fellow has never worked in retail before. "For a man with no experience," he says, "you are certainly asking a high wage."

"Well, sir," the applicant replies, "the work is much more difficult when you don't know what you're doing."

EMPLOYER: I thought you requested yesterday afternoon off to go see your dentist.

EMPLOYEE: Yes, sir.

EMPLOYER: Then why did I see you coming out of the stadium with a friend?

EMPLOYEE: That was my dentist.

How many penguins does it take to fly an airplane?

None. Penguins can't fly.

Burt had a problem with oversleeping and was always late for work. His boss threatened to fire him if he didn't do something about it. So Burt went to his doctor, who gave him a pill and told him to take it before he went to bed. Burt slept incredibly well; in fact, he woke up before the alarm went off. He had a leisurely breakfast and a pleasant ride to work. "Boss," he said, "that pill my doctor prescribed actually worked!"

"That's great," said the boss, "but where were you yesterday?"

> What do you call a seagull
> when it flies over the bay?
>
> *A bagel.*

DAN: I just finished a long run on Broadway.

ZACH: What play were you in?

DAN: Oh, I wasn't in any play. A mugger chased me for ten blocks.

> What kind of snack do little
> monkeys have with their milk?
>
> *Chocolate chimp cookies.*

BARBER: Sir, could you please turn the other side of your face toward me?

CLIENT: Oh, you're finished shaving this side already?

BARBER: Oh, no. I just don't like the sight of blood.

HEARD ANOTHER GREAT JOKE? WRITE IT HERE!

HA HA HA HA

....

....

....

....

....

....

....

....

....

The leader of a large corporation was in a meeting with the board of directors. He presented his plan, although he knew that several of the board would disagree. "All in favor, say, 'Aye,'" said the CEO. "All opposed, say, 'I resign.'"

A Texan was on a flight and began bragging about the property that he owned. "How much property do you own?" asked the man sitting next to him.

"Forty acres," answered the Texan.

"That doesn't sound like all that much," replied the man. "Where is this property located?"

"Oh," said the Texan, "downtown Dallas."

How did the exhausted sparrow land safely?

By sparrowchute.

TEACHER: "If there are a dozen flies on the table and you swat one, how many are left?"

STUDENT: "Uh, just the dead one?"

How does a lion greet the other animals in the field?

"Pleased to eat you."

What did the teddy bear say
when he was offered dessert?

"No thanks. I'm stuffed."

One evening as a mother was preparing dinner, her seven-year-old son came down to the kitchen, crying hysterically. The loving mother bent down and said, "Honey, what's wrong?"

"Mom," he said, "I just cleaned my room."

"Well, I'm very proud of you," she replied. "But why on earth would that make you cry?"

Her son looked up through his tears and said, "Because I still can't find my snake!"

Why did the firefly do well on the test?

Because it was very bright.

Why do bakers work so hard?
Because they need the dough.

JOB SEEKER: I'm here in reply to your ad for a handyman.

POTENTIAL EMPLOYER: And you are handy?

JOB SEEKER: Couldn't be handier. I live right next door.

Why didn't the fly go near the computer?

Because he was afraid to get caught in the Web.

One afternoon, a twelve-year-old boy was taking care of his baby sister while his parents went to town to go shopping. The boy decided to go fishing, but he had to take his baby sister along.

"I will never do that again," the boy told his mother later that evening. "I couldn't catch a thing! I didn't even get a bite."

"Oh, next time I'm sure your sister will be quiet and not scare the fish away," his mother said.

"That's not it," the boy grumbled. "She ate all the bait."

A man was interviewing for a job. "And remember," said the interviewer, "we are very keen about cleanliness. Did you wipe your shoes on the mat before entering?"

"Oh, yes, sir," replied the man. The interviewer narrowed his eyes and said, "We are also very keen about honesty. There is no mat."

What happened to the cat that swallowed a ball of wool?

It had mittens.

A store manager overheard one of his salesmen talking to a customer. "No, sir," said the salesman. "We haven't had any for a while, and it doesn't look like we'll be getting any soon."

The manager was horrified and immediately called the salesman over to him. "Don't you ever tell a customer we're out of anything! Now, what did he want?"

"Rain," answered the salesman.

> **Why did the giraffe graduate early?**
>
> *He was head and shoulders
> above the rest.*

The owner of a large factory decided to make a surprise visit and check up on his staff. As he walked through the plant, he noticed a young man doing nothing but leaning against the wall. He walked up to the young man and said angrily, "How much do you make a week?"

"Three hundred bucks," replied the young man. Taking out his wallet, the owner counted out three hundred dollars, shoved it into the young man's hands, and said, "Here is a week's pay—now get out and don't come back!"

Turning to one of the supervisors, the owner asked, "Just how long had that lazy kid been working here?"

"Oh, he doesn't work here," said the supervisor. "He was just delivering a pizza."

Larry had never cooked a day in his life, but thought he'd like to surprise his wife with a special dinner on her birthday. He went out to the barn, selected a chicken, plucked it, and popped it into the oven.

An hour later he discovered he hadn't turned the oven on. As he opened the door, the chicken sat up and said, "Look, Mister, can you either turn on the heat or give me back my feathers?"

> **What is a lion's favorite food?**
>
> *Baked beings.*

A site foreman had ten very lazy men working for him, so one day he decided to trick them into doing some work for a change. "I have a really easy job today for the laziest one among you," he announced. "Will the laziest man please raise his hand." Nine hands shot up. "Why didn't you put your hand up?" he asked the tenth man.

The guy answered, "It was too much trouble."

> ### What happened when the lion ate the comedian?
>
> *He felt funny.*

A persistent salesman was going door-to-door, and he knocked on the door of a woman who was not happy to see him. She told him in no uncertain terms that she did not want to hear his sales pitch and slammed the door in his face. To her surprise, however, the door did not close; in fact, it flew back open. She tried again, pushing on it as hard as she could, but met with the same result. The door bounced back open a second time. Convinced that this pushy salesman was sticking his foot in the door, she reared back to give it a slam that would teach him a lesson, when he said, "Ma'am, before you do that again, I would suggest you move your cat."

> ### What do you call a sleeping bull?
>
> *A bulldozer.*

SON: "I have good news and bad news."

MOM: "What's the good news?"

SON: "I captured a snake as long as the bathtub."

MOM: "What's the bad news?"

SON: "It just escaped from the bathtub."

The customer wanted to buy a chicken and the butcher had only one in stock. He weighed it and said, "This one's a beauty. That will be $4.25."

"Oh, but that isn't quite large enough," said the customer. The butcher put the chicken back in the refrigerator, rolled it around on the ice several times, then placed it back on the scale again.

"This one is $5.50," he said, adding his thumb to the weight.

"Oh, that's great!" said the customer. "I'll take both of them, please."

What did the farmer call the cow that would not give him any milk?

An udder failure.

Just before Thanksgiving, the teacher asked her kindergarten class, "What do you have to be thankful for?"

One youngster answered, "I'm thankful I'm not a turkey!"

A man at the construction site was bragging that he was stronger than anyone else. He began making fun of one of the older workmen. After several minutes, the older worker had had enough. "I'll bet that I can haul something in a wheelbarrow over to the other building that you won't be able to wheel back."

"Okay," the young man replied. "Let's see what you've got."

The older man reached out and grabbed the wheelbarrow by the handles. Then he looked at the young man and said with a smile, "All right. Get in."

Did you hear about the duck that was flying upside down?

It quacked up.

> **What do you call cattle with a sense of humor?**
>
> *Laughing stock.*

A father was teaching his son to admire the beauties of nature. "Look, son," he exclaimed, "isn't that sunset a beautiful picture God has painted?"

"It sure is, Dad," responded the youngster enthusiastically, "especially since God had to paint it with his left hand."

The father was baffled. "What do you mean, son? His left hand?"

"Well," answered the boy, "my Sunday school teacher said that Jesus was sitting on God's right hand."

Farmer Brown had been injured in an accident. Now he was in court, hoping to gain compensation.

The insurance company's lawyer asked the farmer, "Didn't you say at the scene of the accident, 'I'm fine'?"

Farmer Brown responded, "Well, I can tell you what happened: I had just loaded my favorite horse, Sally, into the—"

"I didn't ask for details," the lawyer interrupted. "Just answer the question: Did you not say, at the scene of the accident, 'I'm fine'?"

Farmer Brown said, "Well, I had just gotten Sally into the trailer, and I was driving down the road—"

The lawyer interrupted again, saying, "Judge, I am trying to establish the fact that, at the scene of the accident, this man told the officer that he was fine. Now, several weeks after the accident, he is trying to collect insurance money. I believe he is a fraud. Please tell him to simply answer the question."

The judge, though, was curious about the answer Farmer Brown was trying to give. "I'd like to hear what he has to say about Sally," the judge said.

Farmer Brown thanked the judge and proceeded. "Well, as I was saying, I had just loaded Sally, my favorite horse, into the trailer and was driving her down the high-way when a huge semi-truck ran the stop sign and smacked my truck right in the side.

"I was thrown into one ditch, and Sally was thrown into the other," he continued. "I was hurting real bad and didn't want to move. But I could hear ol' Sally moaning and groaning. I knew she was in terrible shape just by her groans."

"Soon, a police officer came on the scene. He could hear Sally moaning and groaning, so he went over to her. After he looked at her, he took out his gun and shot her between the eyes. Then the officer came across the road with his gun in his hand and looked at me.

"The officer looked at me and said, 'Your horse was in such bad shape I had to shoot her. How are you feeling?'"

There was a man who owned a giant gorilla and, all its life, he had never left it on its own. But there came a time that he needed to go on a business trip and had to leave his gorilla in his next-door neighbor's care. He explained to his neighbor that all he had to do was feed his gorilla three bananas a day at three, six, and nine o'clock. But he was never, ever, ever to touch its fur.

The following day the man came and gave the gorilla a banana and studied it, thinking, Why can't I touch its fur? There didn't seem to be any harm in it. Every day the man looked for a little while longer, never understanding why he couldn't touch the animal's fur.

About a week later, he was so curious that decided he was going to touch the gorilla. He passed it the banana and very gently brushed the back of his hand against its fur.

The gorilla went wild. It jumped up and down, and then began running toward the man. Terrified, the man turned and dashed through the front door, over the lawn, down the street, and into his car, driving off at high speed. In the rearview mirror, he could see the gorilla keeping pace, lumbering right behind him.

The man drove until the car's engine began to sputter and stopped. So he jumped out and ran farther down the street, climbed over a brick wall into someone's front garden, and hauled himself up an apple tree. He looked back to find the gorilla right behind him, beating its chest.

The man, now screaming, jumped down and ran back into the street. He turned into a narrow alley, thinking he'd lost the beast when, suddenly, a giant shadow appeared on the street ahead. The gorilla!

The animal lumbered down the alley, directly toward the man, who was now paralyzed with fear. Its dark eyes burning, its powerful teeth bared, the gorilla raised its mighty hand over the man's head. Then it tapped his ear and said, "Tag! You're it!"

What animal says, "Baa—baa—woof"?

A sheepdog.

BOSS: "You drive nails like lightning."

CARPENTER: "Pretty fast, huh?"

BOSS: "Nope. You never hammer the same place twice."

What do you call a cow with a twitch?

Beef jerky.

Two little skunks, one named In and one named Out, wanted to go play. Their parents told them they could, but an hour later, only Out came back.

"Hasn't In come in?" asked Father Skunk.

"Out went out with In but only Out came back in," said Mother Skunk.

"Well, Out," said Father, "you better go out and find In and bring her in."

So Out did. And only a few moments later, he returned with his wayward sister.

"Ah, good," said Mother Skunk, pleased. "How did you find her?"

Out smiled. "Instinct," he said.

HEARD ANOTHER GREAT JOKE? WRITE IT HERE!

Why was the cat so small?
Because it only drank condensed milk.

Three turtles—Norm, Sonny, and Bart—decide to go on a picnic. Norm packs the picnic basket with cookies, drinks, and sandwiches. The picnic site they've chosen is ten miles away, and it takes the turtles ten days to get there. By the time they arrive, all three turtles are exhausted. Norm unloads each item from the basket. He takes out the sodas and says, "Sonny, please give me the bottle opener."

"I didn't bring the bottle opener," Sonny says. "I thought you packed it."

Norm gets worried. He turns to Bart. "Bart, do you have the bottle opener?"

Naturally, Bart doesn't have it, so the turtles are ten miles away from their home without soda. Norm and Sonny plead with Bart to return home and retrieve it, but Bart refuses, knowing that the two turtles will eat all of the food by the time he gets back. Somehow, after about two hours of begging, the turtles manage to convince Bart to go, promising that they won't touch the food.

So Bart sets off down the road, slowly and steadily. Twenty days pass, but Bart has not returned. Norm and Sonny are confused and hungry, but a promise is a promise. Another day passes, and still no Bart, but a promise is a promise. After three more days pass without Bart in sight, Norm starts getting restless. "I need food!" he cries.

"No!" Sonny retorts. "We promised." Five more days pass. Sonny realizes that Bart probably stopped at the Burger King down the road, so the two turtles weakly lift the lid, get a sandwich, and prepare to eat their meal.

Suddenly, Bart pops out from behind a rock and says, "Just for that, I'm not going."

What is worse than a giraffe with a sore neck?

A centipede with athlete's foot.

Knock-knock.
Who's there?
Dune.
Dune who?
Dune anything in
particular this
afternoon?

"I came face-to-face with a lion once. And can you believe, I found myself alone and without a gun."

"What did you do?"

"What choice did I have? First, I tried looking straight into his eyes, but he slowly began to creep toward me. I moved back, but he kept coming. I had to do some quick thinking."

"So how did you get away?"

"I just left him and passed on to the next cage."

What do you call a dinosaur that steps on everything in its way?

Tyrannosaurus wrecks.

An archeologist found a coin dated 62 BC and immediately declared it a fraud. How did he know it wasn't real?

BC stands for "Before Christ." This dating system wasn't used until after Christ had been born.

What do you call a mouse that hangs out with a bunch of pythons?

Lunch.

It was a boring afternoon in the jungle, so the elephants decided to challenge the ants to a game of soccer. The game was going well, with the elephants beating the mighty ants ten goals to zip, when the ants gained possession. The ants' star player was advancing the ball toward the elephants' goal when the elephants' left back came lumbering toward him. The elephant trod on the little ant, killing him instantly. The referee stopped the game. "What do you think you're doing? Do you call that sportsmanship, killing another player?"

The elephant sadly replied, "I didn't mean to kill him—I was just trying to trip him up."

When Carl went away on vacation, his brother Ben promised to take care of his cat. The next day, Carl called Ben to see how the animal was doing.

"Your cat is dead," said Ben, matter-of-factly.

"Dead?" said the stunned Carl. "Why did you have to tell me like that?"

"How should I have told you?" asked Ben.

"Well," said Carl, "the first time I called, you could have broken it to me gently. You could have said my cat was on the roof, but the fire department was getting her down. The second time I called, you could have told me the cat fell out of the fireman's arms and broke its neck. The third time I called, you could have said that the vet did every-thing he could, but Fluffy passed away. That way it wouldn't have been so hard on me."

"I'm sorry," said Ben.

"That's all right. By the way, how's Mother?"

"She's up on the roof. . ." said Ben.

How did the scientist invent bug spray?

She started from scratch.

One day a father was driving with his five-year-old daughter, when he honked his car horn by mistake. "I did that by accident," he said.

"I know that, Daddy," she replied.

"How did you know that?"

"Because you didn't holler at the other driver after you honked it."

What do you call a blind dinosaur?

Do-you-think-he-saurus.

"It's so simple! You simply learn to walk pasta da refrigerator without stopping, and pasta da cookie jar, and pasta da cupboard. . ."Two friends went hunting for moose in Canada every year. Each time they were flown out to the marshland in a small bush airplane.

After landing them at their site, the pilot said, "I'll be back to pick you up in five days, and you can only return with you two, your gear, and one moose."

In five days when the pilot landed to pick them up, he found that the men had two moose. He was livid. "I told you only one moose! It's impossible to fly out with the weight of two."

The men said, "But we were here last year, and that pilot took us with two moose, so we thought maybe you could too."

The pilot said, "I'm the best pilot in this country, so if he can do it, I can too."

They stuffed everything into the small plane, closed the door, and took off. They made it up fine, until they came to a tree at the end of the runway and suddenly crashed right into the top of it. Moose, gear, and men went in all directions. When one of the hunters came to, he looked around and said, "Max, where are we?"

The other said, "I'm not sure, Frank, but I think it's about 150 yards farther than we got last year."

> **What did Noah say as he was loading the ark?**
>
> *"Now I herd everything."*

Andy came to work limping like crazy. One of his coworkers noticed and asked Andy what happened. "Oh, nothing," Andy replied. "It's just an old hockey injury that acts up once in a while."

"Gee, I never knew you played hockey," the coworker responded.

"I don't," explained Andy. "I hurt it last year when the referee put my favorite player in the penalty box. I put my foot through the television screen."

> **What do you call two spiders who just married?**
>
> *Newlywebs.*

A city man, tired of the rat race, decided to give up the city life, move to the country, and become a chicken farmer. He purchased a nice, old chicken farm.

He soon discovered that his next-door neighbor was also a chicken farmer. The neighbor came to visit one day and offered, "Chicken farming isn't easy. To help you get started, I'd like to give you one hundred chickens."

The new chicken farmer was elated. Three weeks later the new neighbor stopped by to see how things were going. The new farmer said, "Not very well. All one hundred chickens died."

The neighbor, astonished, said, "Oh, I can't believe that! I've never had any trouble with my chickens. I'll give you a hundred more."

Another three weeks went by, and the neighbor stopped in again. The new farmer said, "You won't believe it, but the second hundred chickens died too."

Astounded, the neighbor asked, "What did you do to them? What went wrong?"

"Well," said the new farmer, "I'm not quite sure. But I think maybe I'm not planting them far enough apart."

HEARD ANOTHER GREAT JOKE? WRITE IT HERE!

....
....
....
....
....
....
....
....
....

AMANDA: "Daddy, does money really talk?"

DAD: "No, honey. It goes without saying."

A man brought a rabbit, a frog, and a chicken to a talent agent's office. As the agent watched with indifference, the frog drank from a glass of water while the rabbit danced around the chicken and performed somersaults.

Just as the agent was about to tell the man to take his animals and leave, the rabbit bowed and said, "Thank you and good night!"

"That's amazing!" said the agent. "The rabbit is hired."

"But what about the frog?" asked the man.

"The frog doesn't have any talent; I want the rabbit," replied the agent.

"But the chicken—" he began.

"No chicken, I want the rabbit only!" the agent insisted.

The following week the agent got the rabbit an appearance on a TV variety show. When it was introduced, the rabbit hopped onto the stage, cleared its throat, and then silently walked off.

"What happened?" the agent asked the owner. "The rabbit didn't say a word!"

"No," said the owner. "The rabbit doesn't talk."

"But last week in my office I heard it—"

"I was trying to tell you."

"Tell me what?"

"About the chicken. He's a ventrilo-quist."

> **Which letter of the alphabet is an island?**
>
> *T—you find it in
> the middle of "water."*

A panda bear walked into a restaurant and ordered a sandwich. When he received the sandwich, he ate it and then took out a gun, shot a hole in the ceiling, and left the restaurant.

A policeman caught up with the panda and told him he had broken the law. The panda bear told the policeman that he was innocent and, if he didn't believe him, to look in the encyclopedia. The policeman got a reference book and looked up "panda bear."

The entry read, "Panda Bear: Eats shoots and leaves."

One day a mime was visiting the zoo and attempted to earn some money as a street performer. But as soon as he started to draw a crowd, the zookeeper seized him and dragged him into his office. Rather than telling the mime not to perform on zoo property, however, the zookeeper reported that the zoo's most popular attraction, a gorilla, had passed away and the keeper feared that attendance at the zoo would decline. He asked the mime if he would be interested in employment, dressing up as the gorilla until they could find another one. The mime pondered the offer and accepted.

The following morning, he donned the gorilla suit and climbed into the cage before the zoo opened. When the crowds began to gather, the mime found that he'd stumbled onto an incredible job opportunity. He was able to sleep all he wanted, play all day, and make fun of people. The crowds were much bigger than they ever had been when he was a mime.

Before long though, the crowds began to tire of him, and he became bored just swinging on the trees in his cage. He discovered that the visitors were paying more attention to the lion in the next cage. Not wanting to lose his status as the zoo's most popular attraction, he climbed to the top of his cage, crawled across the partition, and hung from the top of the lion's cage. Of course, this enraged the lion, but the crowd loved it.

This practice went on for some time. The mime in the gorilla suit kept teasing the lion, the lion kept roaring, the crowds grew larger, and the mime's income kept increasing. Then, one horrible day, as he was hanging above the furious lion, the mime lost his grip and fell.

The mime found himself face-to-face with the lion, which prepared to pounce. The mime was so terrified that he began to run around the cage with the lion following close behind. The crowd roared its approval.

At last, the lion caught up to the gorilla and pounced. The mime found himself on his back, looking up at the irate lion and began yelling, "Help me!"

Immediately, the lion placed his paw over the mime's mouth and said, "Be quiet! What are you trying to do, get us both fired?"

SCOTTY: "Are you a lawyer?"

ATTORNEY: "Yes."

SCOTTY: "How much do you charge?"

ATTORNEY: "A hundred dollars for four questions."

SCOTTY: "Isn't that awfully expensive?"

ATTORNEY: "Yes. What's your fourth question?

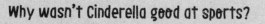

Why wasn't Cinderella good at sports?

Because she had a pumpkin as her coach!

A man was riding his horse down a bridle path when a dog walking down the path said, "Hello."

Surprised, the man said, "I didn't know dogs could talk!"

The horse said, "Neither did I."

A fifth-grade class had behaved abominably at an assembly program, and at the end the school principal announced sternly that there would be no outdoor recess for the remainder of the week. As he turned from the podium, from the middle of the crowded assembly hall came a shout: "Give me liberty or give me death!"

"Who said that?" demanded the principal, wheeling about. There was a short silence.

Then another anonymous voice called out, "Patrick Henry?"

Three animals were having a disagreement over who was the best: The first, a hawk, claimed that because of his ability to fly, he was able to attack anything repeatedly from above, and his prey didn't have a chance. The second, a lion, based his claim on his strength—none in the forest dared to challenge him. The third, a skunk, insisted he did not need either flight or strength to ward off any creature. As the trio argued, a grizzly bear came along and swallowed them all. . . hawk, lion, and stinker.

Timmy was in the garden filling in a hole when his neighbor peered over the fence. Intrigued with what the young boy was up to, he politely asked, "What are you up to there, Timmy?"

"My goldfish died," said Tim tearfully, without looking up, "and I've just buried him."

The neighbor was concerned. "That's an awfully big hole for a goldfish, isn't it?"

Timmy pressed down on the top of the mound then replied, "That's because he's inside your cat."

What is the best type of story to tell a runaway horse?

A tale of whoa.

Knock-knock.
  Who's there?
Arnold.
  Arnold who?
Arnold friend you
haven't seen for years.

A duck hunter was looking to purchase a new bird dog. When he found a dog that was able to walk on water to retrieve a duck, he knew he had to look no further. He was certain that none of his friends would ever believe in his new dog's abilities, so he decided to break the news to a cynical friend of his by taking the man hunting.

On the shore of the lake, a flock of ducks flew by. The dog's new owner fired, and one duck fell. The dog responded by jumping onto the water. He proudly trotted across the lake to retrieve the bird, only getting his paws wet.

The skeptical friend watched the demonstration but didn't say a word.

Later, as they were driving home, the hunter asked his friend, "Did you happen to notice anything unusual about my new dog?"

"Of course," grumbled the friend. "He can't swim."

HEARD ANOTHER GREAT JOKE? WRITE IT HERE!

A boat has a ladder that has six rungs. Each rung is one foot apart. The bottom rung is one foot from the water. The tide rises at twelve inches every fifteen minutes. High tide peaks in one hour. When the tide is at its highest, how many rungs are under water?

None. The boat rises with the tide.

An auto mechanic in the hospital was chatting nervously with his surgeon while being prepped for an operation. "Sometimes I wish I'd gone into your line of work," he told the doctor. "Everything you doctors do is so cut and dried and tidy. With me, I spend half a day taking an engine apart and putting it back together, and it seems I always have a couple of parts left over."

"Yes," said the surgeon. "I know the feeling."

Why do white sheep eat more grass than black sheep?

Because there are more of them.

Two men were fishing in stormy weather. They suddenly were thrown off the boat and found themselves in rough water, with sharks swimming around them. As the sharks began to argue over which got their pick of the fishermen, the largest shark swam over and offered to help.

The psychiatrist was surprised to see a tortoise come into his office. "What can I do for you, Mr. Tortoise?" asked the psychiatrist.

"I'm terribly shy, Doctor," answered the tortoise. "I want to be cured."

"No problem. Hopefully I can soon have you out of your shell."

Which composer is squirrels' all-time favorite?

Tchaikovsky. He wrote "The Nutcracker."

Ole got a new cell phone, and on his way home on the freeway, he called his wife, Lena. "Hello, Lena. I'm calling you from the freeway on my new cell phone."

Lena says, "Be careful, Ole. The radio says that some nut is driving the wrong way on the freeway."

Ole says, "Some nut, my eye. There are hundreds of them!"

Little Tony was in his uncle's wedding. As he came down the aisle during the ceremony, he carefully took two steps, then stopped and turned to the crowd. When facing the congregation he put his hands up like claws and roared loudly. So it went, step, step, turn, roar, step, step, turn, roar, all the way down the aisle. As you can imagine, the congregation was near tears from laughing. By the time little Tony reached the altar, he was near tears too. When later asked what he was doing, the boy sniffed and said, "I was being the Ring Bear."

What has two hands but no arms?

A clock.

BOY: "Could you sell me a shark?"

PET SHOP OWNER: "Why do you want a shark?"

BOY: "My cat keeps trying to eat my goldfish, and I want to teach him a lesson."

"I like the statistics of your quarterback, Evans," a pro scout told a college football coach. "What's your opinion of him personally?"

"Good skills. Sort of a prima donna, though."

"How do you mean?"

"Well, let's just say when he makes a big play, he's all about personal responsibility. When he gets sacked, all about bad luck."

I am cracked; I am made. I am told; I am played. What am I?

A joke.

ART: "Did you hear the concert on the radio last night?"

KERI: "My radio won't come on at night."

ART: "What's wrong with it?"

KERI: "It's an AM radio."

"I've had horrible indigestion for the past two days," a patient said.

"And what have you been doing for it?" asked the doctor.

"Taking an antacid twice a day and drinking nothing but milk," said the patient.

"Good—exactly what I would have suggested myself," the doctor said. "That'll be fifty dollars."

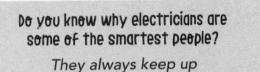

Do you know why electricians are some of the smartest people?

They always keep up with current events.

It had been snowing for several hours when an announcement came over the college campus intercom: "Will the students who are parked on University Drive please move their cars promptly? We must begin plowing."

Fifteen minutes later, there came another announcement: "Will the nine hundred students who went to move thirty-four cars please return to class?"

Knock-knock.
Who's there?
Atch.
Atch who?
Sorry you have a cold.

If ten cats are on a boat and one jumps off, how many are left?

None—they're all copycats.

A teenaged girl had to stay at her friend's overnight. She was unable to call her parents until the next morning. "Mom, it's Caroline. I'm fine. My car broke down last night, and by the time I got to Julie's house it was well past midnight. I knew it was too late to call. Please don't be mad at me!"

By now, the woman at the other end of the phone realized the caller had the wrong number. "I'm sorry," she said, "I don't have a daughter named Caroline."

"Oh, Mom! I didn't think you'd be this mad!"

Mack paid 650 dollars for his gold watch. It was rustproof, shockproof, magnet proof, fireproof, and, of course, waterproof. There was only one thing wrong with it: He lost it.

Did you hear about the lamb that called the police?

He had been fleeced.

The high school band was nervous. So was the new music teacher. As the band members were preparing for their first concert, the teacher told the kids that if they weren't sure of their part, just to pretend to play. When the big night arrived, the proud parents waited expectantly. The teacher brought down the baton with a flourish, and lo, the band gave forth with a resounding silence.

HEARD ANOTHER GREAT JOKE? WRITE IT HERE!

HA HA HA HA

A nonagenarian was interviewed by a local newspaper reporter. "Do you have a lot of great-grandchildren?" the reporter asked.

"To tell the truth," confessed the matriarch, "I expect they're all pretty ordinary."

Knock-knock.
Who's there?
Howard.
Howard who?
Howard is it to
lift a piano?

A man waited at a garage as mechanics scoured his car engine, trying in vain to pinpoint the problem. At length, a parrot in a corner cage sang out, "It's the thermostat."

"We've already checked the thermostat," grumbled one of the mechanics.

"It's the fan belt," the parrot ventured.

"No problem with the fan belt," said the other mechanic.

"It's the water pump," said the parrot.

"It's not the water pump!" shouted the first mechanic, exasperated.

The man was astounded by this exchange. "I've never heard of a bird so intelligent," he said.

"He's completely worthless," countered the second mechanic. "He'll talk your ear off, but he doesn't know the first thing about car engines."

An elderly gentleman had serious hearing problems for a number of years. He went to the doctor and was fitted for a set of hearing aids that allowed the man to hear perfectly. The elderly gentleman went back in a month to the doctor, and the doctor said, "Your hearing is perfect. Your family must be really pleased you can hear again."

The gentleman replied, "Oh, I haven't told my family yet. I just sit around and listen to their conversations. I've changed my will five times!"

What do you get if you cross a snowman with an alligator?

Frostbite.

Once upon a time, there was a clever thief charged with treason against the king and sentenced to die. However, the king decided to be a little merciful and let the thief choose which way he would die. Which way should he choose?

He should choose to die of old age.

"What kinds of papers do I need to travel to Europe?" a youth asked a travel agent.

"Basically, a passport and a visa."

"I have the passport, but no visa. Do you think they'll accept Mastercard instead?"

What do you call a sick alligator?

An illigator.

Farmer Adams was bragging to farmer Black. "I really had a fine day at the market. Guess how many watermelons I sold?"

"'Bout half, I s'pose."

"Half? Half what?"

"Half as many as you're about to claim."

DAD: "I think Junior's planning to become an astronaut."

MOM: "What makes you think so?"

DAD: "He spends every day sitting in a chair, staring into space."

These days many people get their exercise by jumping to conclusions, flying off the handle, dodging responsibility, bending the rules, passing the buck, stirring up trouble, shooting the bull, digging up dirt, slinging mud, throwing their weight around, beating the system, and pushing their luck.

What do you call a group of mice in disguise?

A mousequerade party.

TED: "What's this?"

JANE: "It's dessert. I made it."

TED: "What do you call it?"

JANE: "That's pound cake, silly!"

TED: "Oh. I can see why."

JANE: "What do you mean?"

TED: "I'll need a hammer to pound out the lumps."

MRS. GREEN: "My daughter's marrying a military man—a second lieutenant."

MRS. GRAY: "So, she let the first one get away?"

Henry knelt in front of his girl Henrietta and pleaded, "I've told you before and I'll tell you again: I just can't live without you."

"Yeah, I heard you the first time, and all the other times," she replied. "I would think you'd be dead by now."

Why did the lamb like its computer?

It was ewe-ser friendly.

There was once a lazy alligator that roamed the banks of the river. Whenever a boat passed him, those onboard would be sure to keep their hands inside the vessel, because it was known that he was always looking for a handout.

Why did the farmer call his pig "Ink"?

Because it was always running out of the pen.

> ### What do you get when you cross a robber and a shark?
>
> *A bite out of crime.*

Two street people were being entertained watching a teenager try to park a car across the street. The space was plenty big, but the driver just couldn't maneuver the car into it. Traffic was jammed. Angry drivers honked, further flabbergasting the poor youth. It took a full five minutes before the car was in place.

"That," said one of the idlers, "is what you call paralyzed parking."

> ### What does a chipmunk get when it rains?
>
> *Wet.*

A lady aboard a cruise ship was not impressed by the jazz trio in one of the shipboard restaurants. When her waiter came around, she asked, "Will they play anything I ask?"

"Of course, Madam."

"Then tell them to go play shuffleboard."

What do polite prisoners say when they bump into someone?

"Pardon me."

BRETT: "Do you have holes in your socks?"

JIM: "Certainly not!"

BRETT: "Then how do you get your feet in them?"

What did the judge say when the skunk came in to testify?

"Odor in the court!"

Getting away from their high-stress jobs, May and Trey spend relaxing weekends in their motor home. When they found their peace and quiet disturbed by well-meaning but unwelcome visits from other campers, they devised a plan to assure their privacy. Now when they set up camp, they place this sign on their RV door: INSURANCE AGENT. ASK ABOUT OUR TERM-LIFE PACKAGE.

Why did the ram fall over the cliff?

He didn't see the ewe turn.

GUIDE: "I never guide hunters anymore, just fishermen."

HUNTER: "Why?"

GUIDE: "I've never been mistaken for fish."

What can you hold without touching it?

Your breath.

Ancient Roman magicians used an ingenious method for walking through solid walls. What was it?

A door.

Where do ants go on vacation?

Frants.

BIG SISTER: "Mom says babies are expensive."

BIG BROTHER: "Yes, but think how long they last."

How do you get down off an elephant?

You can't—you get down off a goose.

"What's the most difficult age to get a child to sleep regularly?" a new mother asked an older veteran of child rearing.

"About seventeen years."

HEARD ANOTHER GREAT JOKE? WRITE IT HERE!

HA HA
HA HA
HA

....

....

....

....

....

....

....

....

FATHER: "How are your grades, Peter?"

PETER: "They're underwater, Dad."

FATHER: "What do you mean, underwater?"

PETER: "They're below C level."

"I just returned from Germany and had the most wonderful time," bubbled Ginger to her friends.

"I thought before you left, you said you were having trouble with your German," Melody said.

"Oh, I spoke fluently. It was the Germans who had trouble with it."

"We received our uniforms today," a recruit wrote to his mother from boot camp. "It made me feel very proud, although the pants are a little too loose around the chest."

> **How does a bee get to school?**
> *It takes the buzz.*

Knock-knock.
Who's there?
Midas.
Midas who?
Midas well sit down.

A Sunday school teacher was reading a Bible story to her class. "The man named Lot was warned to take his wife and flee out of the city, but his wife looked back and turned to salt."

A little boy softly asked, "What happened to the flea?"

What is the difference between a fly and a bird?

A bird can fly but a fly can't bird.

FRED: "Don't you wish life were like television?"

TED: "I can't answer that now."

FRED: "Why not?"

TED: "I'm on a commercial break."

If at first you don't succeed, skydiving is definitely not for you.

Patient: "Doc, what do you recommend for an insomniac like me?"

Doctor: "A good night's sleep."

Where do birds invest their money?

In the stork market.

A policeman watched suspiciously as a man stepped out of a van, holding his hands about two feet apart. The man hurried down the street; the policeman followed. At the entrance to a building supply store, the suspect—hands still apart—waited until a customer came through the door. He darted through the open door behind the other person, seemingly afraid to touch the door with either hand. The officer quietly entered the store behind him, just in time to hear the suspect tell a clerk, "I need half a dozen three-by-fours cut exactly this long."

JUDGE: "The last time I saw you, I told you I didn't want to ever see you again."

DEFENDANT: "I told that to the policeman, but he didn't believe me."

What did Delaware do when Mississippi lent Missouri her New Jersey?

I don't know, Alaska.

TEACHER: "Why is the Mississippi such an unusual river?"

STUDENT: "Because it has four Is and can't see."

A baseball team scored four runs in one inning, but not one man reached home. Why not?

It was a girl's team.

What do you have if there are one hundred rabbits standing in a row and ninety-nine take a step back?

A receding hare line.

MARIA: "What would you do if you were being chased by a runaway tractor-trailer truck at 70 miles an hour?"

KARL: "Eighty."

A woman has seven children; half of them are boys. How can this be possible?

All the children are boys.

A lawyer and his doctor friend were working out at the gym. "I come here to exercise, but people are always asking me for advice," the doctor complained to the lawyer. "What do you think I should do?"

"Well," said the lawyer, "the next time you give advice, send a bill."

A few days later, the doctor opened his mail and found a bill—from the lawyer.

What do you call a bird that's been eaten by a cat?

A swallow.

A lad went to an auto parts store and asked for a seven-ten cap. All the clerks looked at each other, and one said, "What's a seven-ten cap?" He said, "You know, it's right on the engine. Mine got lost somehow and I need a new one."

"What kind of a car is it on?" the clerk asked.

"My 2000 Toyota," he replied.

"Well, how big is it?"

He made a circle with her hands about three-and-a-half inches in diameter.

The clerk asked, "What does it do?"

"I don't know, but it's always been there."

At this point, the manager came over. He handed the lad a notepad and asked him if he could draw a picture of it. The customer carefully drew a circle about three-and-a-half inches in diameter. In the center he writes, "710."

The manager, looking at the drawing upside down, walked to a shelf and grabbed an OIL cap.

What do you get if you cross a centipede and a parrot?

A walkie-talkie.

What sign does a nuclear scientist post on the office door when he leaves for vacation?

Gone Fission.

An optometrist examining an elderly patient asked, "Can you read the fifth line on the chart?"

"No."

"How about the fourth line?"

"No."

"Hmm. Try the second line."

"I can't read that one, either."

"Surely you can read the first line."

"Truth is, I've never learned to read."

Why did the dermatologist hurry to the jail?

Everyone was breaking out.

A police officer was escorting a prisoner to jail when the officer's hat blew off down the sidewalk. "Would you like me to get that for you?" asked the prisoner.

"You must think I'm stupid!" said the officer. "You just wait right here while I get it."

HEARD ANOTHER GREAT JOKE? WRITE IT HERE!

HA HA HA HA

A criminal said to the judge, "Your Honor, I'm not guilty. I know I can prove it if you'll just give me some time."

"Sure," replied the judge. "Ten years. Next!"

> **What did the baby porcupine say when it backed into the cactus?**
>
> *"Is that you, Mommy?"*

MOTHER: "Kids, what are you arguing about?"

DAVID: "Oh, there isn't any argument. Lisa thinks I'm not going to give her half of my candy, and I think the same thing."

> **What did the termite do when she couldn't carry the twig on her own?**
>
> *She hired an assist-ant.*

CHUCK: "My doctor said I had to give up playing the drums."

CLUCK: "Why?"

CHUCK: "He lives in the apartment below me."

Sydney: "I must have sneezed fifty times today. Do you think there's something in the air?"

Allen: "Yes—your germs!"

Why were the squirrels sent to the principal's office?

Because they drove the teacher nuts.

A police officer saw a lady driving and knitting at the same time, so after driving next to her for a while, he yelled, "Pull over!"

"No!" she called back. "It's a pair of socks!

What kind of tests are dental students good at?

True or floss.

A man brought his dog to a veterinarian's office. The animal was quite stiff and seemed, to all appearances, dead. But the man wanted to make sure. So the vet examined the corpse thoroughly and pronounced with certainty that the dog had indeed passed away. The man, very upset, asked, "Is there nothing at all you can do? I have to be absolutely certain little Morty is gone before I can begin to deal with it and find peace."

The vet thought a moment, then whispered to an assistant, who went into another room and returned momentarily with a live cat. The cat was placed on the table beside the dog and sniffed the corpse from one end to the other. Then it hopped down from the table and walked back into the other room.

"No question whatsoever," the veterinarian said. "Morty is dead." The vet then wrote out a bill for 200 dollars.

"I don't understand," the man said in dismay. "You're charging me 200 dollars to verify the death of my dog?"

"Not exactly," the vet explained. "My examination was fifty dollars. The other 150 is for the cat scan."

What did the meteorology student say about his final exam?

"It was a breeze with only a few foggy patches."

What do you call a grizzly bear with no teeth?

A gummy bear.

"I guarantee," said the salesman in the pet shop, "that this parrot will repeat every word it hears." A customer bought the bird but found that the parrot wouldn't speak a single word. However, the salesman didn't lie. How is this possible?

The parrot was deaf.

A teacher asked, "Who was the first brother to fly an airplane at Kitty Hawk, North Carolina? Was it Orville or Wilbur?"

"Orville!" shouted one student.

"Wilbur!" shouted another.

"They're both Wright," said a third.

> **What kind of umbrella do people carry on a rainy day?**
>
> *A wet one.*

"Can you carry a tune at all?" the grumpy talent agent asked the final person trying out after a long day of auditions.

"I'll let you judge that for yourself." The person auditioning confidently launched into a terrible, loud rendition of a well-known popular song. "Well, what do you think? Can I carry a tune?"

"Yes," said the agent. "Please carry it out and close the door behind you."

> **What do you call a litter of young dogs that have come in from the snow?**
>
> *Slush puppies.*

FERN: "Oh, I wish I'd listened to my mother."

IVY: "Why? What did she tell you?"

FERN: "I don't know, I wasn't listening."

Two turtles were slowly moving down the road when one was struck in the head by a falling coconut. His friend, afraid that the turtle had lost his memory, rushed his injured companion to the emergency room.

The next day, the friend asked to speak with the doctor. "How is his memory?" asked the concerned friend.

"He's better," responded the doctor. "In fact, I'm happy to tell you that he has turtle recall."

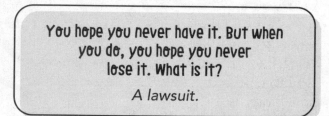

You hope you never have it. But when you do, you hope you never lose it. What is it?

A lawsuit.

PATIENT: "Doctor, I don't know what's wrong with me—I hurt all over. If I touch my shoulder here, I hurt, and if I touch my leg here, I hurt, and if I touch my head here, I hurt, and if I touch my foot here, I hurt."

DOCTOR: "I believe your finger is broken."

Knock-knock.
Who's there?
Juneau.
Juneau who?
Juneau I was your
next door neighbor?

I am used to bat with, yet I never
get a hit. I am near a ball, yet it
is never thrown. What am I?

Eyelashes.

GAMBLER 1: "I finally found a foolproof way to come back from Las Vegas with a small fortune."

GAMBLER 2: "Tell me—quick!"

GAMBLER 1: "Go there with a large fortune."

What would you get if you crossed an
eight–foot snake with a five–foot snake?

Silly, snakes don't have feet!

HEARD ANOTHER GREAT JOKE?
WRITE IT HERE!

HA HA
HA
HA

....
....
....
....
....
....
....
....
....

Two prisoners were commiserating. "What are you in here for?" asked one.

"Stealing a truckload of cement."

"Catch you red-handed?"

"Yeah, the evidence was pretty concrete."

PATIENT: "Doctor! Something's wrong! I'm shrinking!"

DOCTOR: "Take it easy, sir. You'll just have to be a little patient."

A horse is tied to a four-foot rope, and five feet away is a bail of hay. Without breaking the rope or chewing through it, the horse was able to get to the bail of hay. How is this possible?

The other end of the rope wasn't tied to anything.

What do you call a sleeping dinosaur?

A bronto-snore-us.

I can be cool, but I am never cold. I can be sorry, but I won't be guilty. I can be spooked, but I can't be anxious. I can be sweet, but I don't include candy. I can be swallowed, but I will never be eaten. What am I?

Words with double letters.

A college junior was proudly showing off his new apartment to his friends. He led them into the living room. "What are the big brass gong and hammer for?" one of his friends asked.

"That is my talking clock," he replied.

"How does it work?" his friend asked.

"I'll show you," the student said and proceeded to smash the gong with the hammer.

Suddenly, from the other side of the wall, a voice yelled, "Knock it off! It's 1:00 a.m.!"

What's the difference between a fish and a piano?

You can't tuna fish.

Knock-knock.
Who's there?
Dime.
Dime who?
Dime to tell another one of these knock-knock jokes!

How do you keep a skunk from smelling?

Hold its nose.

The manager of a large city zoo was composing a letter to order a pair of animals. He sat at his computer and typed, "I would like to order two mongooses, to be delivered at your earliest convenience." He stared at the screen, focusing on the odd-looking word mongooses. Then he deleted the word and added another, so that the sentence now read: "I would like to place an order for two mongeese, to be delivered at your earliest convenience." Once more he stared at the screen, this time analyzing the new word, which seemed just as strange as the original one. Finally, he deleted the whole sentence and started all over. "Everyone knows no zoo should be without a mongoose," he typed. "Please send us two of them."

Upon entering a little country store, a stranger noticed a sign reading: DANGER! BEWARE OF DOG, posted on the glass door. Inside, he noticed a harmless old hound dog asleep on the floor beside the counter. He asked the store manager, "Is that the dog folks are supposed to beware of?"

"Yup, sure is," he replied.

The stranger couldn't help but smile in amusement. "That certainly doesn't appear to be a dangerous dog to me. Why did you post that sign?"

"Well," the owner replied, "before I posted that sign, people kept tripping over him."

What do you call a cow that has just given birth?

Decalfinated.

Knock-knock.
Who's there?
Deluxe.
Deluxe who?
Deluxe Ness Monster.

Where do sheep get their hair cut?
At the baa-ber shop.

Knock-knock.
Who's there?
Quacker.
Quacker who?
Quacker 'nother
bad joke and
I'm outta here!

Why did the fraction want to go on a diet?
It wanted to reduce.

The dentist was straightforward with his patient. "Now, this may hurt a bit. We're going to have to give you a shot of local anesthesia." The patient took the shot in stride, and after the anesthesia had taken effect, the dentist began to drill. Later, job done, he let the patient out of the chair. The patient turned before leaving and remarked, "Now, this may hurt a bit. I don't have the money to pay. . . ."

The transatlantic flight to England was half-way across when the pilot came on the intercom with a casual message to the passengers: "You may have noticed a slight change in the sound of the engines. That's because we've had to shut down Engine Two temporarily. There's no cause for concern; we have three more engines in fine condition. But there'll be a slight delay. Our expected time of arrival has been changed from 2:14 p.m. to 2:45 p.m. Sorry for any inconvenience that may cause."

An hour later the pilot was back on the intercom, chuckling softly. "Folks, this is the first time I've ever experienced this, and I never thought it would happen, but we seem to have lost power in Engine Four. No problem in terms of safety, but we'll have a further delay. We now expect to arrive at Heathrow International at 3:30 p.m."

And a little while later he was back at the mike, still trying to sound reassuring but with an edge in his voice. "You won't believe this, but Engine One seems to be on the blink, and we've decided it's wise to shut it down. This is a weird situation, but not really alarming. We can easily finish the flight with one engine, although we'll be flying substantially slower.

We now anticipate arriving around 4:25." One passenger turned to another and mumbled, "If that last engine goes out, it'll be next Tuesday till we get to England."

> **Why was the chicken sent to the principal's office?**
>
> *Because it kept pecking on the other kids.*

It had been a very long day, and the mother had had it up to the eyebrows with problems and commotion. "If you don't turn down that rap music," she shrieked to her teenaged son, "I'll go absolutely bananas!"

"It may be too late," her son said. "I turned it off fifteen minutes ago."

> **Why can't goats eat round bales of hay?**
>
> *Because they need three square meals a day.*

HEARD ANOTHER GREAT JOKE? WRITE IT HERE!

HA HA HA

HA

....
....
....
....
....
....
....
....
....

POLICE OFFICER: You are charged with allowing your dog to chase a man on a bicycle.

MAN: That's crazy. My dog doesn't even know how to ride a bicycle.

Two gas company servicemen were out checking meters in a suburban neighborhood. They parked their truck at the end of the alley and worked their way to the other end. At the last house, a woman watched out her kitchen window as they checked her gas meter. When they were finished checking the meter, the older of the two challenged his younger coworker to a race back to the truck. As they came running up to the truck, they realized a woman was huffing and puffing right behind them. They stopped and asked her what was wrong. In between breaths, she explained, "When I saw the two of you check my meter, then take off running, I figured I'd better run too!"

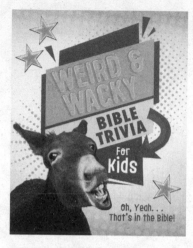